On the Wrong Side of Just About Everything, But Right About It All

Dale Crowley Jr.

Printed by Campbell Copy Center
Harrisonburg, Virginia

Publisher
The King's Business Ministries
P.O. Box One - Washington, DC 20044-0001

Marketing and Distribution
Brandywine House Publications
Brandywine, Maryland
P.O. Box 638 - Cheltenham, MD 20623
703-980-8055

*On the Wrong Side of Just About Everything,
But Right About It All*
by Dale Crowley Jr.

Printed in the United States of America

ISBN 1-59781-670-1

Unless otherwise indicated, Bible quotations are taken from the King James Version.

Dedication

❖⇒◯⇐❖

I dedicate this book to those who gave me daily deadlines, constant pressure, and the enormous opportunity to broadcast the best possible messages to the most important city in the world, Washington, D.C.

I am referring, of course, to radio station WFAX founders and owners, the late Lamar Newcomb, his wife Genevieve, and their daughter Doris who is now President and General Manager, to Program Director Roy Martin, to Chief Engineer Henry Stewart, to Operations Director R.C. Woolfenden, and to Public Service Director Don Karnes.

And I owe a lot to my dear father and mother, who nurtured and maintained a very close friendship with the Newcombs. This has been of great value and blessing to me in my professional relationship with WFAX through the years.

Without the positive influence of WFAX Radio 1220, I would not have produced the unique messages contained in these pages, because I always wanted to do my best for the reputation of this great station (Although 16 chapters, over 50 "Kings Business," "Sound Doctrine Hour," and "Focus on Israel" broadcasts make up this book.)

Indeed, my WFAX colleagues have shown me courtesy, understanding, encouragement, and patience, enabling me, by the grace and in the will of God, to continue on for so long. You see, just as there were mighty efforts to have my father's program eliminated from the WFAX program schedule, two powerful organizations tried to have me silenced as well. So I have good reason to honor those who have played a vital role in the publication of *On the Wrong Side of Just about Everything, but Right about It All.*

Their reward will be great.

TABLE OF CONTENTS

⊷⟞⟝⊶

FOREWORD

⋆⇒◉⇐⋆

Collections of radio sermons don't usually receive the highest acclaim, but I make no apology for these that follow.

I have prepared and broadcast thousands of 15-minute messages to millions of listeners through the years here in the Washington/Maryland/Virginia area (and now nationwide and worldwide on www.wfax.com), all reflections of my lifelong belief in the inerrancy of the word of God, and its power to change the lives of people and nations.

The few messages that I have selected for this book are special for two reasons:

First, they make frequent reference to one of the most sinister and destructive schemes of Bible interpretation ever to invade the church of our Lord Jesus Christ, but embraced by multitudes of unsuspecting, sincere Christians. This scheme is known most and popularly as Scofield dispensationalism. (A corollary and outcome of this definition is that these messages therefore reveal many of the disagreements that I have had with my fellow evangelicals and fundamentalists. Some have even tried to bring my radio broadcasting to an end.)

Before I get to the second reason why this selection of radio messages is special, I must assure my readers that I was once, and still am an expert on the dogmas of dispensationalism. I was exposed to them in church, Sunday School classes, Bible conferences, and Bible college. I actually created a Larkin style chart (better than any of Larkin's) for teaching purposes at my pastorate in Elizabeth City, N. C. In fact, I was expecting someday to be a recognized authority on Scofield dispensationalism. (So to you who feel led to teach me what I need to know about Scofieldism, forget it. Been there, done that.)

The second reason why this selection of radio messages is special is that they have gone through a process of improvement over many years. Some messages began as extemporaneous, then from comprehensive notes, then from word-for-word manuscripts. Then frequently I would do another version for publication in periodicals that welcome my radio broadcast messages.

Finally I want my readers to understand that I have not endeavored to refine these radio messages to the highest level of journalistic standards. Many sentences and paragraphs, even pages retain their original radio broadcast conversational ambience. As in radio broadcasting, there are repetitions of points made earlier. I frequently use the conversational style, "Dear friends," "Dear listeners," and sometimes, where a radio broadcast has become a published article, "Dear readers."

In short, I have not wanted to sacrifice a more informal and engaging speaking style of communication for an absolute adherence to literary consistency. Please understand.

Above all, our Lord Jesus Christ said, "I am the truth." "The truth shall make you free."

I am grateful that I have been liberated from the dominion of the "father of lies," and transferred into "the Kingdom of His dear Son." My highest hope for the messages that follow is that multitudes of readers will accept the truth with respect to the controversies and "shibboleths," and unsound doctrines and dogmas in Christianity today, and likewise freed.

Dale Crowley Jr.

August 18, 2005
On the day of our 55th wedding anniversary

CHAPTER 1

Survey—Fifteen Indicators of Exposure to Dispensationalism, And Seven Israels

*F*riends, let's begin this broadcast of "The King's Business/Sound Doctrine Hour" with a survey. Or we might call it a questionnaire, or a quiz. It is my hope and objective that this survey will help you, my listeners, better understand the system of Bible interpretation known as dispensationalism.

The basic meaning of dispensation is administration, or management. In its broadest religious sense, dispensation refers to the way, or ways by which God manages His creation, especially mankind. (Catholics have a special, more specific meaning for dispensation.) Dispensationalism, as I refer to it frequently in my radio broadcast and publication ministries, is a way of interpreting the Bible in order to identify eras, or periods of God's management of sinful mankind, during which He has provided a variety of ways of redemption. C.I. Scofield identified seven such dispensations, six of which are unbiblical and heretical. I refuse to take valuable time and space to list and refute them, because the only way sinful man has ever been redeemed and justified before God is "by grace through faith."

It is important that we understand and expose as many of Scofield's dispensational errors as we possibly can in order that only biblical truth will remain.

I am happy that I can remind you that my father, who began this Gospel radio broadcast ministry on June 9th, 1941, was not a dispensationalist. Though he held to two or three teachings of Scofield dispensationalism, he refused to accept or teach the vast array of dispensational unsound doctrine. He knew instinctively from his study of God's word for over sixty years that there was a lot wrong with it.

And I want to remind you too, that as I attack dispensationalism in my radio broadcast ministry, there are many listeners who are thankful that there is someone who has the insight and courage to speak out against this false system of Bible interpretation. On the other hand, there are those who have gotten very angry with me, believing that Scofield's notes are just as inspired as the scripture printed above them. They have refused to contribute to the support of this radio ministry, even though they would otherwise like to. Opposition to dispensationalism is just too much for them to handle.

But I am not alone. Recently I read in a Christian publication that certain Dallas Theological Seminary professors are in the process of "destroying dispensationalism." Yes, believe it or not, there are, inside that Mecca of dispensational interpretation, a number of honest Bible scholars who are working toward its demise.

Moreover, several years ago I read a comprehensive article by two of these Dallas Theological Seminary professors about obvious weaknesses and contradictions of dispensationalism. So, I am happy to report this morning that that movement is continuing, and continuing to grow in that hotbed of dispensational error. Dallas Theological Seminary—an otherwise good seminary—is from where most of the dispensational error has been disseminated throughout the nation and the world for many years. It has influenced hundreds of Bible colleges, thousands of churches, and millions of Christians worldwide to accept a multitude of unbiblical heresies.

So to help you understand what dispensationalism is, how the dispensationalists claim that God is managing mankind from era to era, and to help you understand this dispute that is raging throughout the land, I will list fifteen of the most notorious dispensational teachings. And in order for this list, or survey, to "hit home" with greater impact, I will frame all of the fifteen in terms of my and your possible exposure to them.

Please let this survey be your initiation to On the Wrong Side of Just about Everything But Right About It All.

Then in this first chapter read about the seven Israels. Yes, "Seven Israels."

One of the notorious hallmarks of Scofield dispensationalism is its preoccupation with Israel. Scofield seemed to see Israel behind every bush, so to speak. It is so obvious that Scofield dispensationalism is often characterized as "Israel-First Dispensationalism." The word "Israel" occurs several times in our 15-point survey.

But one of the pitfalls of all discussions of Israel, I have found, is that we do not delineate or identify which Israel, or which aspect of Israel we are talking about. Consequently, such discussions usually end up in confusion, and even hard feelings. For example, in an argument about the place of Israel in the plan of God, Person A may be thinking of the nation of Israel under kings Saul, David, and Solomon, while Person B may be thinking of the little nation of Israel in the Middle East.

So, dear listener and dear reader, please study carefully the seven Israels that appear in the past, present, and future.

SURVEY OF FIFTEEN TEACHINGS OF DISPENSATIONALISM

Teaching No. 1: If you have heard that God's promises to Abraham included special blessings to those who would bless Jews and Israel, but that He would curse those who curse Jews and Israel, then you have been exposed to dispensational error. (Abraham was neither a Jew nor an Israelite.) How can the cult of Israel preachers and politicians spread this error when the Jews didn't emerge as an identifiable people until 1500 years after Abraham? And the twentieth century nation of Israel isn't even mentioned in the Bible.

Teaching No. 2: If you have heard that God decided on seven dispensations (management eras) in which there would be seven different ways for lost sinners to be saved, then you have been exposed to dispensational error. (At the most there are three dispensations: Old Testament, New Testament, and the eternal Heavenly Kingdom.)

Teaching No. 3: If you have heard that God's chosen people include all the rebellious, blasphemous, anti-Christ and anti-Christian Israelites of history and the world today, you have been exposed to dispensational error.

Teaching No. 4: If you have heard that God's Old Testament covenants and promises are a) unconditional (no "ifs," no "thens"), b) that those covenants and promises were carried over into the New Testament era, and c) that they are running parallel to His acts of redemption on behalf of those who are "saved by grace through faith" (Ephesians 2: 8), then you have been exposed to dispensational error.

Teaching No. 5: If you have heard that our Lord Jesus Christ came to this world first and foremost to establish and rule over a Jewish kingdom from a throne in a temple in Jerusalem, then you have been exposed to dispensational error.

Teaching No. 6: If you have heard that our Lord's teachings in the "Sermon on the Mount" (Matthew chapters 5, 6, and 7), and elsewhere in the four Gospels, are not for His church today, but for the "tribulation saints" and Jewish believers during the Millennial Kingdom, then you have been exposed to dispensational error.

Teaching No. 7: If you have heard that our Lord's parable of the fig tree in the "Olivet Discourse" (Matthew 24:32-33) refers to Israel, rather than to the truth that He, our Lord, clearly set forth, then you have been exposed to dispensational error. (What presumption, what effrontery and arrogance, to ignore and discard the divine interpretation by our Lord Jesus Christ of His own parable, replacing it with a foolish dispensational interpretation.)

Teaching No. 8: If you have heard that our Lord Jesus Christ returned to the Father, *not* having occupied the throne of David in accordance with Old Testament prophecies as revealed in Acts 2:25-36 and Acts 15:13-11 (the Apostles cited Old Testament prophecies and their *fulfillment*), then you have been exposed to dispensational error.

Teaching No. 9: If you have heard that the Apostle Paul preached only the "Gospel of the Grace of God," while our Lord preached only the "Gospel of the Kingdom of God," Paul having never preached the "Gospel of the Kingdom of God," then you have been exposed to dispensational error.

Teaching No. 10: If you have heard that our Lord Jesus Christ is coming back seven years before His complete and final return, in order to a) raise the saints of God of all ages from the dead, and snatch away His people from the "Great Tribulation," b) set the stage for both Jewish trouble ("the time of Jacob's trouble") and Jewish evangelism (why anti-Christ would torment the greatest anti-Christs of history is a mystery to me), and c) get ready for a second resurrection and snatching away ("rapture") on the occasion of His "glorious appearing," then you have been exposed to dispensational error. (I remind you, the Bible says nothing about *two resurrections, two raptures,* and *two last days*...but only one of each. And "last" means "last." There cannot be one last day seven years before a second last day.)

Teaching No. 11: If you have heard that in his letter to Titus the Apostle Paul intended to place a seven years period of time between the "blessed hope" and "glorious appearing" ("...the blessed hope and glorious appearing of the great God and our saviour Jesus Christ"), then you have been exposed to dispensational error.

Teaching No. 12: If you have heard that our Lord Jesus Christ will return to establish a Jewish kingdom which he failed to do the first time around, sitting on a throne in a third temple in Jerusalem, and presiding over Old Testament style temple worship, such as sacrifices of lambs, red heifers, etc., then you have been exposed to dispensational error.

Teaching No. 13: If you have heard that the seven churches of Revelation chapters 1, 2, and 3, represent seven different, precise (or perhaps better, *imprecise*) eras of the Christian church over a period of approximately two thousand years, then you have been exposed to dispensational error. (Parenthetically, here dispensationalists are guilty of believing and teaching a monumental contradiction. They aver that the New Testament teaches that our Lord Jesus Christ can return "imminently," that is, at any moment. But in the same breath they say that He will return only at the conclusion of the era of the seventh church at the end of the 2,000 year "church age," at the time of the Laodicean church! It can't be both, my friends.)

Teaching No. 14: If you have heard that the *saints*, mentioned frequently in Revelation chapters 5 through 22, are the so-called "tribulation saints," and *not* members of the church, the body of Christ, then you have been exposed to dispensational error. Nowhere in the book of Revelation does the inspired revelator John identify "saints" as so-called "tribulation saints" as distinct from other New Testament saints. Will we believe the inspired John or the dispensationalists?

Teaching no. 15: If you have heard that at the beginning of the Great Tribulation, immediately after the rapture of the church, 144,000 Jews will be saved, then travel throughout the world preaching the Gospel, bringing multitudes to Christ, and accomplishing in seven short years what the church of Jesus Christ had not been able to accomplish in twenty centuries (all this activity in the midst of the reign of Antichrist!!!), then you have been exposed to dispensational error.

Dear friend, I trust that this short fifteen point survey has helped define *dispensationalism* for you, and that you will be interested enough to read the messages that follow, that feature thorough, point by point explanations and unraveling of not only these fifteen, but many other dispensational teachings as well.

Please keep in mind that one reason these studies are so important is that dispensationalism is divisive. Good men and women have been expelled from churches and organizations because they would not accept it. I myself have been excluded from many groups, fellowships, churches, schools, etc., because of my outspoken and convincing arguments against it.

One more reason why it is so essential to study and be well informed and sure about dispensationalism: It elevates and inflates the importance of Israel—the man, the people, the kingdom, and the modern nation—far beyond what God intended in His revealed word, the Bible. And this has given rise, in turn, to a flood of pernicious beliefs, practices, policies, and events.

SEVEN ISRAELS

Seven Israels are discussed on the "Focus on Israel" and "King's Business" radio programs from time to time. Certain ones of the seven get more attention than others, of course, but all are important.

Since the word "Israel" occurs more than 2,500 times in the Old and New Testament scriptures, it is right for us indeed to "Focus on Israel."

But when they focus on Israel, many of my evangelical and fundamentalist Christian friends do not make a distinction between any of these seven Israels. They teach, preach, and argue about Israel as if every aspect and feature of Israel were one and the same. This leads to great misunderstanding and misinterpretation of scripture.

One of their biggest mistakes, for example, is to equate the 20th century nation of Israel with one or all of the following:

Israel in the wilderness
Israel under Saul, David, and Solomon
Israel the northern divided kingdom
Israel dispersed among the nations

This confusion is the cause of much unhappy and unfortunate disputation among Christians. It is absolutely impossible to discuss the subject of Israel with someone who does not make a distinction between these seven Israels, who uses the word "Israel" to mean only one all-encompassing entity.

There is one more important word of explanation that must be made. Certain of the seven Israels are not entirely distinct and separate from the others. There can be, and is some overlapping.

For example, (1) the people Israel populated the kingdom Israel, (2) throughout history the people Israel who believed God, as Abraham believed God, are also God's spiritual Israel, and (3) the 20th century nation of Israel has citizens who are Israelites ethnically, and who are also, because of their faith, God's spiritual Israel—a three-way overlap.

So here are the seven Israels that we feature in our radio ministry, with a few brief comments on each.

1. *Israel the man.* His name was changed from Jacob to Israel by God Himself. Genesis 32:28. The name Israel sets forth a beautiful truth. It means "Prince with God," or "Warrior for God," or "ruling with God," or some other similar truth.
2. *Israel the family, the people.* These are the immediate family of Israel the man, together with all of his descendants, even to the present time.

"Israel" is not used in this way in the final chapters of Genesis, but beginning with the book of Exodus. Israel the man's descendants are referred to as "the children of Israel." "The children of Israel" occurs twelve times in the first three chapters of Exodus (and throughout scripture, of course), after which we begin to read of the "elders of Israel," and eventually, just simply "Israel" in both the Old and New Testaments.

3. *Israel the kingdom* under Saul, David, and Solomon for 120 years.

This is a very specialized meaning of the word "Israel," and applies for only 120 years of Old Testament history. It encompassed all the areas designated to the twelve tribes, the descendants of the ten sons and two grandsons of Israel.

4. Israel the kingdom, the northern division of the divided kingdom. Following Solomon's death the kingdom of Israel split

into Israel in the north and Judah in the south. At the beginning of the divided kingdom, Israel in the north consisted of everything except the tribe of Judah and her territory. See I Kings 11:31-36. (As time went on, however, Israel diminished in size, with Judah adding portions or all of Simeon, Benjamin, and Dan. The residents of Judah became known as Judeans in both Hebrew and Greek. It is from the word "Judean" that we derived the shortened form in English, "Jew." "Jew" does not occur in the original languages Hebrew or Greek. The word is "Judean.")

Israel fell to the Assyrians in 722 and Judah to the Babylonians in 586.

- - - - - - - - - - - - - - - - - -

During the 400 years between the Old and New Testaments "Israel" existed under definition number 2 above—as the descendants of the twelve tribes—some back in Palestine, some remaining in their captor nations, and some dispersed among the nations. This Israel continued into New Testament times, and even until today.

- - - - - - - - - - - - - - - - - -

5. *Israel the spiritual family of God.* Although Christians for centuries have accepted this spiritual interpretation of Israel, we are now accused of the imagined heresy of "replacement theology."

Let us dismiss this flawed concept for what it is worth—nothing—and go on.

The Apostle Paul prayed for "the Israel of God." (Galatians 6:16) "The Israel of God" cannot possibly mean the multitude of rebellious, unbelieving, unsaved Israelites of all generations. It must mean all those—believing Galatians included—who, like Abraham, believed God and were accounted righteous, salvation made possible through the atoning work of the Son of God, Jesus Christ.

The salvation of "the Israel of God" is explained fully in the ninth, tenth, and eleventh chapters of Romans.

The most astonishing and convincing linkage of Old Testament Israel with the spiritual Israel of the New Testament is Peter's quotation of Exodus 19:5-6: "...ye shall be a peculiar treasure unto me above all people: for all the earth is mine. And ye shall be unto me a kingdom of priests, and an holy nation."

The inspired apostle wrote, "Ye are a chosen generation, a royal priesthood, an holy nation, a peculiar people, that ye should shew forth the praises of him who hath called you out of darkness into his marvelous light" (I Pet. 2:9)

God's spiritual Israel includes both Old and New Testament saints, and the church which His Son, our Lord Jesus Christ established. No other Israel is of any great importance or significance in this New Testament Age of Grace.

6. *Israel the 20th century nation.* In view of the foregoing it can be neither said nor proved that the nation of Israel is the fulfillment of any Old Testament promise or prophecy. The nation of Israel was founded upon Marxist and socialist doctrines. It has passed laws unfavorable to Christian citizens, missionaries, and immigrants. It has conducted the affairs of state in most undemocratic, unjust, and brutal ways. It supports a state religion which elevates the Talmud above the Torah (the five books of Moses). To equate this nation of Israel with anything good and godly in the Bible is a travesty of Biblical interpretation.

7. *Israel in the future.* The Apostle Paul wrote, "And so all Israel shall be saved." (Romans 11:26) The Apostle John wrote that 144,000 "of all tribes of the children of Israel" would be "sealed." "Sealed" speaks of spiritual salvation. (From the context—Rev. 6:12-15 and 7:9-17—it is clear that these sealings take place at the end of the tribulation. Nothing is said about preaching the Gospel to a lost world.)

So we can say boldly that the final and full salvation of Israel in prophecy is the *future destiny* of the spiritual Israel—the people of God of all nations and ages, "the Israel of God"—set forth in number 5 above.

As far as Israel in the future is concerned, there is not one scripture that teaches that our Lord Jesus Christ will reign over a physical Israel—Israelites running around on earth in bodies of flesh and blood—in His millennial kingdom.

CHAPTER 2

Left Behind—
God's People, Not the Wicked

⁕══◑◐══⁕

Friends, let's give high priority to one of the foremost deceptions of these end times of the last days, spread like a pernicious virus throughout planet earth by Tim LaHaye's Left Behind series of books. Tens of millions of these books have misled hundreds of millions of our fellow man, and made Tim LaHaye a millionaire.

Let me say simply and plainly, "Believe and be saved, watch and pray, and prepare, as Noah did, to be LEFT BEHIND!"

Noah and his family were left behind, saved! The wicked of his day were taken away, lost! So Tim LaHaye has it 100 percent wrong, 180° backwards!

Our Lord Jesus Christ taught, in Matthew 24:28,37-40, that God's judgment is like the flood of Noah's day, that takes away the wicked, leaving behind the good. Like buzzards that take away rotten, stinking flesh, leaving behind the living, the clean, and healthy. Like calamities that take away some, leaving behind others.

So it is clear that Scofield, Lindsey, McGee, Falwell, Robertson, Hagee, LaHaye, et. al., who teach contrary to what our Lord taught are deceived, and they have become renowned deceivers of the end times.

The Bible, from Genesis to Revelation, is clear and consistent on this fundamental truth: With only a very few exceptions (Enoch for example), the unbelieving unsaved are taken away in the judgment of God, while the believing saved are left behind to experience His blessing, protection, and salvation.

The only end-times "catching away" of God's people mentioned in His word is the one that occurs immediately following the resurrection of His people of all ages. It is the "caught up" of I Thess. 4:17, popularly known as the "rapture," which is immediately preceded by the resurrection of "the dead in Christ." These two events are the "gather together" of Matthew 24:31, occurring on the "last day," not seven years before.

Nowhere in the word of God is it taught that seven years before the last day there will be a day of resurrection and "rapture" on which God's people will be "gathered together," while the wicked are left behind. This scenario is unbiblical, unsound doctrine.

Noah and his family were left behind saved. Noah and his family's escape into the ship that he had built is not a type of the "rapture" of the church, as LaHaye and multitudes of dispensational false prophets have taught. The ark and those aboard never left the earth. They were protected from God's wrath, and lived to serve Him.

Moreover, Noah never preached an "any moment" deluge, flood, judgment and salvation. The ship had to be finished. And he and his family did not vanish in a "rapture." The wicked looked on as God protected His own.

So the Left Behind series of books are full of unsound doctrine, fiction, and heresy. God's people are the ones who are left behind.

The Bible study that follows sets forth what fifteen of the most well known, beloved passages of the New Testament say about the events of the Second Coming of our Lord Jesus Christ. Notice that these fifteen scriptures are in perfect harmony with one another, but all in conflict with the Scofield et. al. dispensationalist deceivers.

The Return of Christ on the Last Day
According to
Matthew 24

1. Deception will prevail—vv. 4,5,11,24
2. End-time events will be shortened on behalf of the "elect" —the church, the body of Christ—v.26
3. The Second Coming of Christ will not be "secret"—v.26 (compare "secret rapture")
4. The Second Coming will be spectacular, like lightning, noisy, with trumpet and natural disasters—vv. 27,29,31
5. The lost will be **TAKEN**; the elect **LEFT BEHIND**; then "gathered together"—v.31

6. The parable of the fig tree refers to the occurrence of the preceding 15 signs. The interpretation of this parable has nothing whatsoever to do with Israel. It is near blasphemy to ignore and discard our Lord's interpretation of His own parable—then substitute one's own private interpretation—vv. 32-33

7. The Second Coming is likened to the judgment of Noah's day: The lost are taken; the saved are left behind—vv. 37-39

8. Those who are not ready will be surprised—vv. 43-44. Those who are ready do not know the hour, but they will not be surprised.

Note: The notion that the resurrection and "rapture" are events that precede the events of Matthew 24, and that the prophecies of Matthew 24 are for the Jewish tribulation saints only IS PURE, UNADULTERATED DISPENSATIONAL HERESY. Matthew 28:20 says "all things," "not some things."

The Return of Christ on the Last Day
According to
John 6

1. Jesus will raise His own from the dead on the last day—vv. 39-40,44, not seven years before the last day.

2. Jesus will raise His own from the dead on the last day—v. 54, not seven years before the last day.

Note: "Last" means "last." There cannot be two last days. Pre-tribulation rapture heresy demands two resurrections and two raptures, separated by seven years. The Bible clearly teaches only one resurrection and one "rapture," on the LAST DAY.

The Return of Christ on the Last Day
According to
John 11

1. Jesus taught the resurrection of the dead —v. 23. Martha believed the resurrection of the dead on the last day—v. 24

The Return of Christ on the Last Day
According to
John 14

Jesus promised simply, "I will come again and receive you unto myself." v. 3 The Son of God knew that His disciples would be in the resurrection preceding the "rapture." (Peter was particularly aware that he would be in the resurrection, not the "rapture." Why? See John 21:18-19. Peter did not and could not teach an at any-moment pre-tribulation secret "rapture" seven years before the last day. See II Peter 1:14)

The Return of Christ on the Last Day
According to
Acts 1

The key words are "in like manner."—v. 11 Jesus will return to earth (not stopping "in the air"), visibly, physically (resurrection body) and audibly, and after the assigned task of world evangelization has been accomplished. An "any-moment" return was impossible.

The Return of Christ on the Last Day
According to Acts 17

The day of judgment by the risen Christ —the last day— has been "appointed." v.31 Paul did not preach an any-moment, pre-tribulation secret "rapture" in which the wicked would be **"LEFT BEHIND."**

The Return of Christ on the Last Day
According to
I Corinthians 15

1. The resurrection of the dead will occur at Christ's "coming," at the "end" vv. 23 and 24.
2. The resurrection of the dead will occur at the last trump" — v. 52

Note: "Last" means "last." There cannot be two last trumps. There is only one "last trump," on the LAST DAY, the great day of resurrection, "rapture," and judgment. I Corinthians 15 does not teach two resurrections and two "raptures."

The Return of Christ on the Last Day
According to
I Thessalonians 4

1. The resurrection will occur first. Then the "catching away" vv.15-16.
2. The Second Coming will be a resounding event, with a "shout," "the voice of the archangel," and the "Trump of God"—v.17.

Note: The Second Coming of Christ will be neither silent nor secret.

The Return of Christ on the Last Day
According to
I Thessalonians 5

Note: I Thessalonians 4 and 5 speak of the same last day Second Coming events. The chapter division was not in Paul's letter to the Thessalonians.

1. The "day of the Lord"—the great day of resurrection, "rapture," and judgment—comes as a "thief in the night" only to those who are not ready—vv. 2-4.
2. God's people will be exempt from His wrath, that is, from His "day of the Lord" judgment on a wicked world, just as Noah and his family were spared His wrath on the wicked world of his day—v. 9.

Note: Nowhere in scripture are God's people promised to be exempt from the tribulation of the world. "Wrath" and "tribulation" are two distinct words in the Greek language of the New Testament.

The Return of Christ on the Last Day
According to
II Thessalonians 1

1. The Thessalonians mistakenly thought that the "day of Christ" (2:2) had come, or was coming soon. Paul said, "No." His return will be with angels, with fire, and with vengeance against the wicked—vv. 7-9 He told them they couldn't possibly miss it.
2. On the same day of judgment against the wicked, Christ will be "glorified" and "admired" in His saints—v.10.

NOTE: Paul did not tell the Thessalonians, who were awaiting the Second Coming, to look for a secret, silent "rapture." Paul described the return of Christ as a spectacular, resounding event in which the lost would be TAKEN, while the saved would be LEFT BEHIND to meet Him in the "gathering together" of II Thessalonians 2:1.

The Return of Christ on the Last Day
According to
II Thessalonians 2

"The day of Christ" ("the "day of the Lord," "the last day") will be preceded by a **falling away**, and **the revelation of the man of sin, Antichrist**. Paul assured the Thessalonians that they would observe both before the resurrection and "rapture" of the last day, "the day of Christ." vv. 3-4

The Return of Christ on the Last Day
According to
Titus 2

The day of the "blessed hope," and the day of Christ's "glorious appearing" are the same day, not two different days separated by seven years. The Greek word "kai" in this verse should be translated "even," not "and." The verse should read, "Looking for that blessed hope, even the glorious appearing of the great God and our

Saviour…"v.13 Note: The notion that the "blessed hope" occurs on one last day when the wicked are LEFT BEHIND, and that the "glorious appearing" occurs on another last day, is another dispensational heresy.

The Return of Christ on the Last Day
According to
II Peter 3

1. Just as his Lord did (Matthew 24), Peter linked the world-wide flood of Noah's day to a coming judgment by fire—vv.3-7
2. This coming day of judgment is likened to a period of 1,000 years. (See Revelation 20:27 —"thousand years" mentioned six times) —v. 8
3. "The day of the Lord". . . "a thief in the night" (to those who are not ready)¬v.10
4. "The day of the Lord," "the day of God" (the last day)—judgment day will be accompanied by spectacular, resounding events—vv.10-12

Note: Peter brings together the judgment of Noah's day with the judgment of the LAST DAY—the wicked are TAKEN, the saved are LEFT BEHIND. These momentous events, which will be neither silent nor secret, may span 1,000 years.

The Return of Christ on the Last Day
According to Jude

1. Those whom God saves are LEFT BEHIND. The unbelieving—Egypt and Sodom—are "destroyed," TAKEN—vv. 5-7
2. The coming of the Lord on the day of judgment—the LAST DAY—will be resounding, spectacular—vv.14-15

The Return of Christ on the Last Day
According to Revelation

There are many verses in Revelation regarding the Second Coming of Christ, and how His saints—the elect, the church await and prepare for His return—from 1:7 "Behold he cometh with clouds, and every eye shall see him" to 22:30 "Surely I come quickly." There are also many references to God's judgment against the wicked, while His people, waging spiritual warfare and enduring tribulation, are victorious.

Note: Revelation 4:1 has nothing whatsoever to do with a secret, silent pre-tribulation "rapture" of the church. Such a private, fanciful interpretation is just more dispensational nonsense.

CHAPTER 3

The First Advent of Jesus Christ—Jesus Saviour and King Accepted by Old Testament Believers

*L*et's begin at the beginning.

The men and women of God who lived during the first years of the New Testament era (6 B.C., 5 B.C., 4 B.C., 3 B.C., 2 B.C., 1 B.C., 1 A.D., etc.) were awaiting the coming of their Messiah Saviour, not a king who would establish and rule over a Jewish kingdom. And when they met Him they recognized Him as the promised One.

Those godly Israelites studied and believed the Old Testament scriptures, and therefore possessed an accurate expectation and hope. On the other hand, the ungodly Israelites of that day, who had forsaken Moses and the prophets, possessed an improper, inaccurate expectation, that of an earthly political, temporal Jewish kingdom with a Jewish king. Incredibly, during the past 200 years there has arisen a parallel, analogous system of sound and unsound doctrine concerning both the First Advent and the Second Advent of our Lord Jesus Christ, one emphasizing earthly, worldly events, and one emphasizing heavenly, spiritual events.

One of the great ironies of church history is that today's Bible believers, conservatives, evangelicals, and fundamentalists are, by and large, because of their devotion to Scofield dispensationalism, more in harmony with the early church's Judaistic factions than with the beliefs and ministry of the apostles. They believe and teach, for example, that the covenants and promises of the Old Testament are still in effect for Jews, and that Jesus will come again to sit as king on a throne in Jerusalem presiding over animal sacrifices and ruling over a Jewish kingdom.

It is indeed a curious irony that such unsound, heretical interpretations of scripture, which elevate a temporal Jewish kingdom with a Jewish king over the eternal spiritual Kingdom of God with its true and eternal King, the Son of God, and His church (which is a part of His eternal kingdom), have gained acceptance by so many Christians. In this third chapter of this book of insightful and courageous radio broadcast messages read what first century Bible believing Christians, and twenty centuries of Bible believing Christians have believed and taught about the first Coming of the promised Messiah of the Old Testament, the eternal King, the Son of God, Jesus. Then contrast that with what two centuries of Darby/Scofield dispensationalists have mistakenly believed and taught.

The Gospel radio broadcasts that are featured in this chapter were aired over a period of several Christmas seasons, and deal with many of the same truths. Consequently, you will find considerable repetition of scripture, and historical and doctrinal facts. I could have edited out all the repetitions, but that would have detracted from the spirit of these "live and in person" radio broadcasts.

Every Old Testament prophecy concerning the coming of the Messiah is fulfilled in the birth, life, death, burial, and resurrection of our Lord and Saviour, the Messiah.

("Saviour" means "Jesus." "Messiah" means "Christ.") Most of my readers have seen long lists of those Old Testament prophecies and their New Testament fulfillments.

This truth—the truth of fulfilled prophecy—has certain profound implications which, I am sorry to say, have escaped our 19th and 20th century dispensational "theologians."

First, foremost, and fundamentally, it means that godly Old Testament believers who were living when our Lord was born understood those Old Testament prophecies, and that they believed that the newborn Baby was the very fulfillment of those prophecies. To put it another way, those "transition period" believers who knew and understood Old Testament doctrine did not believe that the newborn Baby had come to establish a physical and secular Jewish kingdom, over which He would reign from Jerusalem.

The second implication of the truth of fulfilled Old Testament messianic prophecies is this: Today's dispensationalist teachers and believers are in agreement with those "transition period" unbelievers who harbored false hopes for a messiah who would establish himself as a physical, secular king over a physical, secular Israel. (Now they say, "His plan was rejected, so He will return to reinstate his kingship and kingdom.")

So this second terrible implication of false dispensational teaching is that our Lord Jesus Christ, the Saviour and Messiah prophesied in the Old Testament *did not* come as "the Lamb of God which taketh away the sin of the world" (John 1:29), to die on the cross and shed his blood for our sins.

So it is clear that today's dispensationalists are on the same side as New Testament era unbelievers. They teach that He had another purpose which was started by the rejection of ungodly Israelites and Jews.

What a travesty this strange dispensational system of biblical interpretation is!

The True Hope of Spiritual Believers

There are clear truths revealed about the hope of true believers in the early chapters of the Gospel narrative...truths that are not at all what the dispensationalists would have us believe.

Joseph and Mary

Joseph and Mary were devout students and believers of the Old Testament. They were expecting a spiritual Saviour and Messiah. The angel said to Joseph, "...thou shalt call his name JESUS: for he shall save his people from their sins." (Matt. 1:21) The angel Gabriel described the coming Messiah in detail: "...and thou shalt call his name JESUS [SAVIOUR]. He shall be great, and shall be called the Son of the Highest: and the Lord God shall give unto him the throne of his father David: and he shall reign over the house of

Jacob for ever and ever; and of his kingdom there shall be no end." (Luke 1:3-33) Neither Joseph nor Mary, nor the Gospel writers ever doubted that those promises were fulfilled.

Zacharias and Elisabeth

Zacharias and Elisabeth were expecting a spiritual Saviour and Messiah. The angel of the Lord promised Zacharias concerning his son John, "And many of the children of Israel shall he turn to the Lord their God to make ready a people prepared for the Lord." (Luke 1:16,17) On the occasion of Mary's visit to Elisabeth, Elisabeth said, "...there shall be a performance of those things which were told her from the Lord." (Luke 1:45) There was never any indication that either Zacharias or Elizabeth was disappointed that the promises to them that their son would be a major participant in God's plan of salvation had been broken.

In his prophecy following the birth of John, Zacharias expressed a spiritual hope in very spiritual terms, such as "Redeemed his people," "horn of salvation," "be saved," "mercy," "holy covenant," "being delivered," "knowledge of salvation unto his people by the remission of their sins," "tender mercy of God," "light to them that sit in darkness," and "the way of peace." Zacharias definitely was not looking for a physical, secular Jewish kingdom!

The Shepherds

The shepherds were given to believe that a spiritual Saviour had come. They believed the angel's announcement of spiritual salvation, "I bring you good tidings of great joy, which shall be to all people. For unto you is born this day in the city of David a Saviour, which is Christ the Lord." (Luke 2:10-11) Notice the words "to all people." It definitely was not a Jewish kingdom that God the Father had in mind.

Simeon and Anna

The "Just and devout" man and eighty-eight year old widow woman who met the holy family in the temple eight days after

Jesus' birth were not looking for a king over a physical, secular Israel. These two devout, godly descendants of Israel met the family and declared that the holy Infant was the promised One of the Old Testament.

Simeon was "Just and devout, waiting for the consolation of Israel." *"Then he took him up in his arms and blessed God, and said Lord now lettest thou thy servant depart in peace according to thy word: for mine eyes have seen thy salvation which thou hast prepared before the face of all the people; a light to lighten the Gentiles and the glory of thy people Israel."* (Luke 2:25-32)

"Anna the eighty-eight year old prophetess coming in that instant gave thanks likewise unto the Lord, and spake of him to all of them that looked for redemption in Jerusalem." (Luke 2:38)

These two good, godly descendants of Israel were being true to their Old Testament heritage. They recognized Jehovah God's expression of love, grace, and salvation in the newborn Christ. They definitely were not looking for a physical secular Jewish kingdom.

John the Baptist

John the Baptist quoted the prophet Isaiah when he announced the *salvation of God* in the person of Jesus Christ. *"All flesh shall see the salvation of God."* (Luke 3:6) *"All the ends of the earth shall see the salvation of our God."* (Isaiah 52:10) John the Baptist had a proper understanding of Old Testament scriptures and prophesies. He definitely was not looking for a physical, secular king over a physical, secular Israel.

Our Lord identified Himself as a Spiritual Saviour and Messiah. Jesus Himself preached to the Jews of His day that the Old Testament scriptures *"are they which testify of me!"* (John 5:39) He said further, *"for had ye believed Moses, ye would have believed me; for he wrote of me."* (John 5:46) In other words those who did not accept Him were not even good Jews, because they had already turned their backs on the writings of Moses! So the Jews who were looking for a physical, secular king to rule over a physical, secular Israel did not understand the plan of God as revealed in the Old Testament, just like today's dispensationalists!

The Apostles Were Well Taught in the Meaning of Old Testament Prophesies

The Apostle Peter would disagree with today's dispensational-ists. Following the healing of the lame man at the Beautiful Gate, Peter cited Old Testament prophecies *five times*, and *not once* did he teach a physical, secular king over a physical, secular Jewish kingdom. This sermon proves beyond any doubt that our Lord had instructed His disciples in the true, spiritual purpose of His coming.

"But those things, which God before had showed by the mouth of all his prophets, that Christ should suffer, he hath so fulfilled...God hath spoken by the mouth of all holy prophets since the world began. For Moses truly said unto the fathers, a prophet shall the Lord your God raise up unto you of your brethren...every soul which shall not hear that prophet, shall be destroyed from among the people. Ye and all the prophets from Samuel and those that follow after...Ye are the children of the prophets...in thy seed shall all the kindreds of the earth be blessed" (Acts 3:18-25)

The Apostle Peter clearly was not preaching that the Israelite and Jewish descendants of Abraham would enjoy a physical, secular kingdom, ruled over by a physical, secular messiah. Today's dipensationalists would sharply disagree with Peter.

Stephen

After quoting extensively from the Old Testament, Stephen the martyr accused the council scholars of unbelief and rebellion against the teachings of the Old Testament. He argued that their refusal of Jesus Christ was consistent with their refusal of the truths of the Old Testament. Stephen did not accuse them of rejecting a physical, secular king over Israel, but of rejecting the Saviour of sinners. He affirmed that God's temple was a spiritual temple: *"Howbeit the most High dwelleth not in temples made with hands; as saith the prophet."* (Acts 7:48)

Stephen accused the theologians and scholars of his day of rejecting not a physical, secular, temporal king—but of *"the Just One."* *"Ye stiffnecked and uncircumcised in heart and ears, ye do always resist the Holy Ghost; as your fathers did so do ye. Which of the prophets have not your fathers persecuted? And they have slain them which showed before of the coming of the Just One of whom ye have been now the betrayers and murderers." (Acts 7:51-52)*

The Jerusalem Council

One of the favorite chapters of the dispensationalists to over-look is Acts 15. In this pivotal chapter the Apostles of our Lord, meeting in Jerusalem, did indeed agree that the prophets prophesied a spiritual Saviour for the whole world, and a spiritual King sitting on a spiritual throne ruling over a spiritual kingdom! *"And to this agree the words of the prophets; as it is written, after this I will return and will build again the tabernacle of David which is fallen down; and I will build again the ruins thereof; and I will set it up: That the residue of men might seek after the Lord, and all the Gentiles upon whom my name is called, saith the Lord, who doeth all these things." (Acts 15:15-17)*

Paul

The Apostle Paul preached the Gospel of this spiritual kingdom from the beginning to the end of his ministry, and he proclaimed our Lord Jesus Christ as the "King eternal." (I Tim. 1: 7) Not one time did Paul even so much as hint that our Lord Jesus Christ came to establish a physical, secular kingdom, that he failed in His mission, or that He decided to postpone it to establish it at a later date.

A great portion of the ministry of Paul was devoted to proving that Jesus Christ was the fulfillment of prophecies of the Old Testament concerning the Messiah.

He argued constantly that the Jews of his day had misunder-stood and rebelled against the plain teachings of the Old Testament scriptures, and as a result were blinded to the love and grace of God revealed in our Lord Jesus Christ. And Paul found that the descendants of Israel whom he could most readily win to Christ were those who feared God and believed the Old Testament. In Antioch, for example, those in the synagogue who believed his sermon on the many links between the Old Testament and the life, death, and resurrection of Christ were saved, while those who did not believe remained rebellious, *"because they knew him not, nor yet the voices of the prophets which are read every Sabbath day." (Acts 13:27) "Now when the congregation was broken up, many of the Jews and religious proselytes followed Paul and Barnabas, who, speaking to them persuaded them to continue in the grace of God." (Acts 13:43)*

To this day, a Jew or descendant of Israel who is true to his Old Testament heritage will come to Jesus Christ. But those, like today's dispensationalists, who held false, unscriptural hopes for a physical, secular king who would reign over a physical, secular Israel, did not believe.

The Songwriters Were Theologically Correct

We all love the beautiful music that speaks of the coming and birth of our Lord Jesus Christ. Many of the songs refer to the newborn Messiah as Saviour and King. The songwriters had their theology right. Here are but a few examples:

"Twas the birthday of a King."
"Joy to the world, the Lord is come; let earth receive her King."
"Hark the herald angels sing, Glory to the newborn King."
"Peace on earth, goodwill to men, from heaven's all gracious
    King."
"Silent night, holy night…Alleluia to our King."
"For the manger of Bethlehem cradles a King."
"Praises sing to God the King, and peace to men on earth."
"Born a King on Bethlehem's plain, Gold I bring to crown Him
    again, King forever, ceasing never, over us all to reign."
"Born a Child, and yet a King, born to reign in us forever, now
    Thy gracious kingdom bring."
"Come and worship, come and worship, worship Christ, the
    newborn King."
"Come, adore on bended knee Christ the Lord, the newborn
    King."

"The King of kings salvation brings, let loving hearts enthrone Him. This, this is Christ the King."

"He surely could have it, 'cause He was the King."

Dispensationalist Temerity

Many, many more songs and hymns of our Christian faith make reference to our Lord Jesus Christ as King, His spiritual kingdom, and the spiritual purpose of His coming. He is King and His kingdom has been established.

What temerity the dispensationalists possess to dispute the prophets, the angels, the faith of Joseph, Mary, Zacharias, Elisabeth, the shepherds, Simeon, Anna, John the Baptist, our Lord Himself, His Apostles, Stephen, Paul, and hundreds of songwriters through the centuries concerning the spiritual purpose of our Lord's First Coming!

Contrary to Darby/Scofield/Lindsey Dogma
THE SON OF GOD CAME TO SAVE SINNERS
"The son of man is come to seek and to save that which was lost." Jesus, Luke 19:10
"Christ Jesus came into the world to save sinners."
Paul, 1 Tim. 1:15

Christmas celebration is one of the strangest of all human activities. Jesus was most likely born in September, certainly not on December 25th. The Bible nowhere instructs us to celebrate His birthday. Most of us celebrate this most important of all birthdays by forgetting Him and giving to others. The name of the holiday—Christmas—is derived from one of the most important Roman Catholic masses of the year, CHRIST MASS. Finally, to add insult to injury, it is said that the pagan winter festival of Saturnalia is the real, historical origin of December 25th celebration.

But all of this does not constitute our biggest problem with our remembrance of the birth of our Lord and Saviour Jesus Christ.

Then what is our biggest problem?

Our biggest problem is with what is known as dispensational-ism, a system of Bible interpretation concocted in Plymouth, England, only about 200 years ago, *following 1800 years of heroic struggle between believers of sound doctrine with the peddlers of unsound doctrine.*

My dear friend and fellow missionary, the late Dr. James R Graham—missionary, theologian, and author—was so alarmed at the blatant deceptions and subtle unbiblical implications of Darby/Scofield/Lindsey dispensationalism, that he wrote a book opposing it entitled, *The New Higher Criticism.* His point was that what the modernists and liberals missed in their cutting up and discarding the inspired word of God, dispensationalists finished off with their "rightly dividing" scripture. ("Rightly dividing" is a mistranslation of the Greek word meaning "cutting straight" or "properly interpreting.")

Dispensational Deceptions
Concerning the Coming of Christ

Let's get right to the point of the headline above: "The Son of God Came to Save Sinners" Luke 19:10

The dispensationalists teach that the Son of God came to offer and establish Himself as an earthly king to rule over God's earthly people, the physical descendants of Abraham, Isaac, and Jacob, known popularly as "the Jews."

Not so. Heresy. Our Lord Jesus Christ came to save sinners. Period.

The dispensationalists teach that devout Israelites ("Jews") were looking for the establishment of such a kingdom with a "Jewish" messiah as king.

Not so. Heresy. Devout, Bible (Old Testament) believing Israelites, such as Joseph and Mary, Zacharias and Elisabeth, Simeon and Anna, and the Galileans Andrew, Peter, James, John, etc., and hundreds of others were looking for a *spiritual saviour* and a *spiritual salvation. All the others, like the dispensationalists, were mistaken.* The dispensationalists teach that we must not spiritualize Old Testament messianic prophecies.

Not so. Heresy. Isaiah prophesied that the coming Messiah Saviour would fill the valleys, level the hills, and straighten the crooked roads. (Isaiah 40) Palestine is still a land of valleys, hills, and crooked roads. The fulfillment of this messianic prophecy is spiritual, not literal.

The dispensationalists teach that our Lord Jesus Christ postponed His cherished Jewish kingdom, and set up His church as a stopgap, temporary, inferior alternative. But they say, He will return to establish the glorious earthly kingdom for his "earthly people," the Jews.

Not so. Heresy. Jesus promised that hell itself would not triumph over His church, and His Apostles agreed that Jesus Christ is now "the eternal King" (I Tim. 1: 16), sitting on the spiritual (nevertheless literal) "throne of David." The Apostles declared in Acts 15:13-17 that the prophecy of Amos 9:11-12 had been fulfilled!

Finally, the dispensationalists teach that when our Lord Jesus Christ gave us the parable of the fig tree in the Olivet Discourse in Matthew 24, he was pointing to the restoration of Israel (whatever that means...return to Palestine?...renewal of "Jewish" government?...a revival of Babylonian Talmudic Judaism?...who knows?)

Not so, Heresy. Our Lord gave us His own divine, authoritative interpretation of His "fig tree" parable. (Read Matthew 24 and see for yourself.) By what authority do any so called Bible teachers— no matter how famous and how popular—have to absolutely disregard the divine words and revelation of our Lord Jesus Christ, and substitute their own foolish notions?

THE SON OF MAN IS COME TO SEEK AND TO SAVE THAT WHICH WAS LOST. CHRIST JESUS CAME INTO THE WORLD TO SAVE SINNERS.

MISSION ACCOMPLISHED
Not Failed or Postponed

The New Testament writers, the church fathers, and 18 centuries of theologians all affirmed that the purposes for which our Lord Jesus Christ came from heaven to earth were all accomplished. There was not one failed or postponed mission.

Not until dispensationalism, pre-tribulation rapturism, and Israel-first theology appeared around 1830 was the total fulfillment and accomplishment of our Lord's First Advent ever questioned.

An interesting Bible study at this time of the year is to note the many references to the birth of the *King*, and His love for and rule over *Israel i*n our so-called Christmas carols. What inspired these statements of faith from the hearts and minds of the songwriters? What was the biblical basis for such poetry? Some outspoken dispensationalists go so far as to voice their objection to such mentions of Israel, the newborn Jesus as King, and especially the combination of the two, Jesus Christ as King over His Israel.

Why? Simply because dispensationalism teaches that our Lord Jesus Christ failed in his mission to become king over Israel, therefore, this failed mission should not be enshrined in our sacred music!

It is important to understand, further, at this season of the year, that one of the driving forces behind many of the strange doctrines and interpretations of the dispensationalists is a false importance assigned to *Old Testament Israel during this New Testament dispensation*. They go so far as to say that restored Old Testament Israel (during the Great Tribulation) will accomplish more in the evangelization of the *world in the absence of the Holy Spirit and in the midst of great tribulation in 7 years than the church of Jesus Christ did with the presence of the Holy Spirit in 2,000 years!*

Preposterous.

And then they accuse me, and simple Bible believers like me, of "replacement theology." That is, we have replaced their future King Jesus, King of Israel, with our present King Jesus, not only the Head of His body, the church, but also the King of His spiritual Israel. We will see from the scriptures below that the Israel-first dispensationalists are the ones guilty of "replacement theology," not we.

So to end this short First Advent Bible study on a positive note, let us list some of the missions accomplished by the coming of the Messiah.

Jesus came as true Israel's true King. "The prince of peace." (Isa. 9:6) "He shall reign over the house of Jacob (Israel) forever." (Lk. 1:33)

He came to save His people from their sins. (Lk. 19:10) "He shall set up an ensign for the nations, and shall assemble the outcasts of Israel." (Isa.11:12) "And she shall bring forth a son, and thou shalt call his name JESUS: for he shall save his people from their sins." (Matt. 1:21)

He established and ascended to the throne of David. "Upon the throne of David, and upon his kingdom, to order it, and to establish it with judgment and with justice from henceforth even for over." (Isa. 9:7, 8) "The Lord God shall give unto him the throne of his father David: and He shall reign over the house of Jacob for ever; and of his kingdom there shall be no end." (Lk. 1:32-33) "I will...build again the tabernacle of David..." (Acts 15:13-17) See also Acts 2:29-36 and Psalm 110:1

He continued His eternal reign and firmly established the Kingdom of God on earth. "My kingdom is not of this world." (John 18:36) "Whose kingdom is an everlasting kingdom." (Dan. 7:27)

He fulfilled all Old Testament prophecies concerning the suffering and glorified Messiah, His death, burial, and resurrection. "The Lord hath laid on him the iniquity of us all." (Isa. 53) "For thou wilt not leave my soul in hell; neither wilt thou suffer thine Holy One to see corruption." (Psalm 16:10 with Acts 2:23-32)

He and his Apostles predicted his Second Coming many times, as well as the collapse and overthrow of the governments of the nations of the world, His day of judgment, and the ultimate victory of life over death, of light over darkness, of good over evil, and of God the Father, God the Son, and God the Holy Spirit over all for all eternity.

MISSION ACCOMPLISHED
Not Failed Or Postponed.

CHAPTER 4

James R. Graham Yes, John N. Darby No

*T*he next few *"right-about-it-all"* chapters address many of the specific errors of the system of Bible interpretation known as <u>*dispensationalism*</u>. *A few introductory paragraphs are essential.*

Dispensationalism is one of seven evil movements that emerged in the 1800s, and that influenced the events of the 1900s tremendously. It could be said that the 1800s (nineteenth century) were the years of Satan's final preparation for the catastrophic spiritual, economic, political, and, military warfares of the twentieth century.

Indeed, all the struggles and losses of Christian civilization in the twentieth century can be traced to these seven evil movements which gained full acceptance by large segments of the populations of civilized nations, and which were further advanced by fanatical devotees of the seven. (It can be demonstrated, of course, that all seven had their roots in the 1600s and 1700s, but the full flowering of these satanic deceptions took place in the 1800s.)

Here are the seven:

<u>*Evolutionism.*</u> *Evolutionism provided a supposed rational and scientific justification to eliminate God as the Creator, Sustainer, and Moral Ruler of His universe. Moral accountability to a higher authority vanished. (The suffix "-ism" goes with evolution, not creation. All Christians should stop using the pair of words, "evolution and creationism," and begin saying "evolutionism and creation.")*

__Higher Criticism.__ This theological movement provided a supposed scholarly justification to reject the doctrine of the divine inspiration and inerrancy of the Holy Bible. (Also known as modernism and religious liberalism.)

__Communism.__ Communism advanced the supposed justification for the overthrow of historical political guarantees, such as the private ownership of property and free enterprise. In Communism an evil end justifies an evil means, such as the enslavement and murder of vast populations in order to establish "better" totalitarian dictatorship.

__Freemasonry and Other Occult New Age Philosophies.__ Although suffering serious setbacks in the 1800s (See Charles Finney's monumental book on Freemasonry.), occultism recovered, and manifested its anti-God, anti-Christ, anti-Trinity rebellion worldwide with great success.

__Progressivism and Humanism in Education.__ Thousands of years of traditional concepts and methods of teaching children were discarded in favor of numerous unproved, untried pedagogical schemes. Progressivism trashed the successful teaching strategies of the past. Humanism removed God from the educational process and made man the center of all knowledge.

__Zionism.__ This seemingly noble movement advanced the supposed right of the Jews of the world to confiscate and "reclaim" property in Palestine, owned for hundreds of years by the Palestinian Arab people. (Even Khazaric Ashkenazi Jews who are not Semites, who never had ancestors in Palestine, and who had no part in the Zion of the Old Testament, were included in this claim and movement.)

__Dispensationalism.__ Dispensationalism is a system of ("rightly") dividing the Bible and God's activities among mankind into pieces, or eras, known among its devotees as *"dispensations," or more understandably, "management eras." This system of biblical interpretation destroys the unity of the Bible, particularly the unity of God's love and grace to mankind for all ages. It vitiates the militancy of Christ's church by advancing reliances on unbiblical dispensational "promises." Dispensationalism also joins hands with Zionism to produce a double assault on God's plan for the end times, that is, it advances a combination of false hopes for both ungodly Jews and an anemic church.*

With roots in 17th century novel prophetic speculation, dispensationalism came into full flower through the zealous efforts of the Plymouth Brethren under the leadership of Bible teachers like John Nelson Darby, C. H. MacIntosh, and C. I. Scofield.

Dispensationalism was the focus of the few hours I spent with Dr. James R. Graham in the spring of 1952. It is my duty before God to share the blessings and teachings of those few hours through the pages of ON THE WRONG SIDE OF JUST ABOUT EVERYTHING BUT RIGHT ABOUT IT ALL.

RESCUED FROM DISPENSATIONALISM BY DR. JAMES R. GRAHAM

I will honor and pay tribute to Dr. James R. Graham, China missionary, educator, and theologian, and share the priceless teachings that he imparted to me so powerfully and convincingly years ago. It is a rule of the Christian life that when God entrusts to us something special from one of His choice servants, it is then our privilege and responsibility to pass it on to others.

Who was Dr. James R. Graham, and what were the circumstances of our meeting?

I will never know all about Dr. Jim, but there are not many left in this world who were as close to him as I was.

During Billy Graham's early years Dr. James R. Graham (no relation) served as one of his closest and most trusted advisors. Dr.

Jim was the son of China missionaries who served with Ruth Graham's parents, the Bells.

So when Billy Graham prepared for the spring 1952 crusade in Washington at the National Guard Armory, he asked Dr. Jim to come over from Taiwan to help.

(It was on the occasion of this crusade that one of the jealous preachers of Washington informed Billy Graham that Dale Crowley, my father, would not be serving on his crusade committee. Billy told that pastor that he could leave the committee if he wished, but Dale Crowley would remain. That was back when Billy Graham still had strong convictions and moral courage.)

Right Start for the Day

One day after the crusade had gotten underway my father told me about a wonderful China missionary, and he asked me to go to the WWDC radio studios at 6:30 the next morning to introduce this missionary, Dr. James Graham, who was a member of the Billy Graham Crusade team, and who would promote the crusade on the Right Start for the Day radio program. Since Mary and I and our 9 month old son David were leaving for Japan in a few weeks, my father thought it would be good for me to meet this experienced China missionary, and be the one to introduce him to the Right Start for the Day radio audience. What a great privilege and opportunity, that I must confess I did not understand at the time.

To this day I can remember my foolish response. I didn't care who James Graham was, nor did I want to get up at 5:30 in the morning to meet him at 6:30 for a radio broadcast at 6:45! But thank God, my father persuaded and prevailed.

Thus began one of the most exciting and satisfying journeys of my life and ministry. Such encounters, dear reader, are not mere happenstance. And, as I have already expressed in this message, I have always believed that I must be a good steward of that momentous, auspicious meeting.

A Two Hour Introduction to Remedial Bible Prophecy and Eschatology

When I met Dr. Graham at WWDC on the corner of Connecticut Avenue and K Street in Northwest Washington I was immediately impressed with his manliness and self-confidence, my kind of preacher, like my father. His scholarship unfolded as we spent the morning together.

The broadcast went well, and I was ready to return home, where Mary and I were making final preparation for our first missionary journey to Japan. (Mary, at 20, holds the record for the youngest missionary wife ever to go to Japan.)

But somehow—I wish I could remember exactly *how*—our parting conversation turned to prophecy and the Second Coming of our Lord Jesus Christ. Dr. Jim knew that I was in a hurry, but he very graciously invited me to his hotel room to discuss these things further. I drove him to his hotel, THE RITZ-CARLTON. A simple young man of 23 in 1952, I was impressed.

Dr. James R. Graham got right down to business, point by point, step by step, demolishing every card in the dispensational house of cards. He zeroed in on the error of the pre-tribulation secret rapture teaching as well as the overall fraud, deception, and heresy of the Scofield *et. at.* system of dispensationalism. He was powerful and convincing that winter morning of 1952.

I was stunned and intrigued. I had no counter arguments. God had given me a questioning, analytical, investigative spirit from birth, so I listened to Dr. Jim respectfully as he attacked every Scofield dispensational notion that I had assimilated from fifteen years of evangelists, Bible conference speakers, and college professors. All I could do was ask questions.

Dr. Jim was a fundamentalist Presbyterian minister, Bible college president, and missionary. He knew the scriptures.

We communicated well, because by that time I had become a young, promising expert in dispensationalism and pre-tribulation rapturism. I knew all the terminology, all the "cards" in the dispensational "house of cards," and all the right questions to ask.

I asked Dr. Graham if he had discussed these things with Billy Graham, and if Billy Graham had received his warnings about dispensationalism and pre-tribulation rapturism. Dr. Jim said, "Yes." (Dear reader, as much as we might admire or criticize Billy Graham, we will never hear him preach dispensational error, including the pre-tribulation rapture of the church. He just does not believe it.)

My Big, Long-Standing Doubt

I had already had one lingering doubt about one of the cardinal doctrines of dispensationalism for several years, the any-moment pre-tribulation rapture of the church. It was this: If the New Testament does indeed teach that our Lord Jesus Christ could have returned to this earth at any moment after He ascended into heaven, then why do prophetic teachers insist that we are now living in the time of Christ's return 20 centuries later, because all the end-of-the-age signs have been fulfilled? These are contradictory, incompatible teachings, and I knew it.

Dr. Jim nurtured that doubt, and then made mincemeat of that particular flaw and foible of the any-moment secret rapture theory. After all, if God the Father, Son, and Holy Spirit are sovereign, then the exact time of our Lord's return has been set, and nothing will change it, not even the return of ungodly Jews to the "Holy Land." (Dear reader, please indulge me a little sarcasm.)

Lasting Friendship and Fellowship

So great was my admiration for Dr. Jim after that auspicious encounter that I followed him and his ministry in Japan, Taiwan, and the U.S. At one point in our friendship he strongly urged me to leave Japan to come to Taiwan to help him in the great ministry of the Bible College he had founded in Taipei, Christ's College.

Truths Confronted in That Two-Hour Introduction to Anti-Darbyism

It would be impossible for me to recollect and pinpoint every doctrine and argument of those two hours, simply because my knowledge of dispensational error began to grow immediately, and has continued to grow until the present day. But the following were surely a part of that first day of liberation. .

This is what I learned about dispensationalism and pre-tribulation rapturism from Dr. James R. Graham on a spring day in 1952:

1. Dispensationalism as a system of prophetic interpretation was (in 1952) only 120 years old, having been developed in Plymouth, England by the Plymouth Brethren under the leadership of John Nelson Darby. (We now know that pre-tribulation rapturism appeared about 50 years earlier in the U.S.) This means that for 1800 years the church of Jesus Christ did not hold to such views.

2. Not all Plymouth Brethren subscribed to these novel teachings. George Mueller, the great giant of faith who trusted in God to provide for his orphanage, and John Tregelles, for example, were ostracized from the Plymouth Brethren fellowship for opposing dispensationalism and pre-tribulation rapturisim.

3. The church historically believed that the Second Coming of Christ would be preceded by a time of terrible suffering— the Great Tribulation. In fact, for 1800 years there were many times in which Christians were certain that Christ's return was imminent, simply because of widespread persecution, as predicted in scripture.

4. "Imminent" means "impending," not "at any moment." Christ's return could never be "at any moment" simply because the Father has set the time, and certain events must take place prior to this great event.

5. Peter, who wrote much about our Lord's Second Coming, did not expect Him to return at any moment, because He told Peter that he would die a martyr in his old age.

6. The dispensational theory that Jesus came to establish a Jewish kingdom is heresy. John the Baptist preached. "Behold the lamb of God that taketh away the sin of the world," and Jesus Himself said, "The Son of man is come to seek and to save that which was lost." Also heretical are all the dispensational teachings that elevate unsaved Jews to a status equal to or above the church of our Lord Jesus Christ. Also heretical are all "Jewish" teachings about the rebuilding of the temple in Jerusalem, the resumption of animal sacrifices, and "kingdom Jews" running around on earth in flesh and blood together with the resurrected saints of God in glorified bodies.

7. The heretical theories about the four Gospels—Matthew, Mark, Luke, John—that certain portions or all of them are so-called "kingdom truth," not for the church today. Dr. Jim pointed out to me how this scheme of things is necessary to the dispensational house of cards in order to eliminate contrary teachings, such as The Olivet Discourse, Matthew chapters 24 and 25.

8. I had my Scofield Bible with me, so Dr. Jim turned right to page 1002 and showed me another gem of dispensational heresy, Scofield's comment on Matthew 6:12, "And forgive us our debts, as we forgive our debtors." According to Scofield, "This is legal ground. Cf. Eph. 4:32, which is grace. Under law forgiveness is conditioned upon a like spirit in us; under grace we are forgiven for Christ's sake, and exhorted to forgive because we have been forgiven." Pure heresy and good example of mistaken, misguided dispensational law and grace dichotomy. (You will not find these heretical interpretations in your new Scofield Bible today. They were officially expunged in the mid 1960s, after misleading millions of trusting, worshipful-of-Scofield Christians.)

9. Another dispensational heresy that Dr. Jim explained to me that fateful morning in the winter of 1952 was the kingdom-church dichotomy. He turned to pages 1010 and 1011 of any Scofield Bible, where Scofield writes about the King's offer of a kingdom, the rejection of the King and His kingdom, and "The new message of Jesus: not the kingdom, but personal discipleship." Pure heresy, twisting of scripture, and travesty of "rightly dividing the word of truth."

This heresy, of course, has vast implications. It means that Calvary's cross was a second thought, Plan Two. It means that if the King and kingdom had been accepted by the Jews there would have been no atonement. And for the future it means, according to Darby, Scofield, Walvoord, Lindsey, et. al. that Jesus must take up where He left off with the rejected Plan One, to establish His coveted Jewish kingdom the first thing following His Second Coming. Pure heresy, twisting of scripture, and travesty of "rightly dividing the word of truth."

Another implication of Scofield's mistaken kingdom-church dichotomy is the notion that while the church has been and is a great failure in the accomplishment of God's purposes on earth, the Jewish kingdom, prepared for by the work of 144,000 Jewish preachers, will be an illustrious success. So what Christ's church could not accomplish in 2,000 years as the body of its divine Head, a company of Jewish tribulation saints will accomplish in a few short years. (Actually, the "sealing" of the 144,000 occurs as one of the events of the sixth seal, at the very close of the Great Tribulation, not at the beginning that the Apostle John is talking about. I will deal with this dispensational deception in a later broadcast.

10. Dr. Jim put the rapture of the surviving church in proper perspective; that is, that it is a relatively minor event following the major event, the resurrection of the saints of God of all ages. The resurrection of God's people on "the last day" is anticipated and prophesied in both the Old and

New Testaments. Countless millions of saints of every century of human history will rise from their graves (and even from such "graves" as atomic annihilation, death at sea, etc.) to meet Christ in the air at His glorious appearing.

Dr. Jim taught me that the word "remain" in I Thessalonians 4:15 means "survive." The implication in the Greek text is that there will not be a great number of Christians who will survive the Great Tribulation. Therefore, compared to the great resurrection that precedes it, the rapture of the church is a minor event.

11. Titus 2:13 did not escape Dr. Jim's scrutiny that momentous morning. I had wondered, but never questioned how the little word "and" in this important scripture could represent seven years; that is, seven years between the "blessed hope" and "glorious appearing," or whether the "blessed hope" and "glorious appearing" were two different events. The explanation is that in the Greek language of the New Testament, just as in English, the word "and" can also mean "even," so that the Apostle Paul is talking about one great event, "the blessed hope, *even* the glorious appearing of the great God *even* our Savior Jesus Christ."

12. One of the most flagrant pre-tribulation rapture subterfuges that Dr. Jim explained to me that day 53 years ago was the "two last days," "two raptures," "two resurrections" implication.

I say "implication" because this teaching is not ever mentioned. It is the "dirty little secret" of dispensationalism.

Six times in the Gospel of John our Lord put the great day of resurrection and judgment on "the last day." (6:39, 6:40, 6:44, 6:54, 11:24, and 12:48) By definition "last" means "last." There cannot be two last days, two raptures, two resurrections, or two Second Coming judgments.

CHAPTER 5

Three Greek Words for the One
Second Coming

*B*efore we proceed from truth number twelve about dispensational error that I learned from Dr. James R. Graham on that early spring morning in 1952, to truth number thirteen and following, it is well that we consider a few more important matters of background.

Someone might ask at this point. "Dale Crowley Jr. why have you waited 50 years to tell us what you learned from Dr. Graham in 1952?

As a matter of fact I have not been quiet about it. I have taught and convinced many these 50 years that the any-moment pre-tribulation secret rapture is a false hope. To be sure, knowing the fanaticism and viciousness of the dispensationalists, I have had to exercise extreme caution.

In a sense I am ashamed of myself for not broadcasting and publishing these important clear and precious truths boldly long ago for all to hear and read. But perhaps now is the best time.

We are living in the end time of the last days. Worldwide lawlessness and deception are on the rise. I will soon be eighty, and may not have many more months or years left to preach and teach the truth of God's word. So perhaps what I am broadcasting and publishing in these series of studies at this time will have a greater impact than at any other time since 1952.

I will mention, in passing, that there are other reasons why I have not taken this daring and momentous step in earlier years. (Such as, for example, that I have less to lose now than at any other time in my life!)

Personal Considerations and Consequences

Dr. Jim warned me, and I learned early on, that America's Christians would not readily receive the truth of scripture on this subject, so thorough had been satanic deception and brainwashing for 120 years.

I found out very soon that Dr. Jim was exactly right. The word got around my many missionary friends in Japan that I was no longer a dispensationalist, or worse, no longer a pre-tribulation rapturist. Dr. James R. Graham was well known in Japan and throughout the Far East, but that didn't protect him or me from the shunning that goes with anti-Scofieldism.

Back here at home I was blacklisted and ostracized by pastors and churches. Although I have never...and will never...deny the Second Coming of our Lord, the post-tribulation rapture of surviving saints, or His millennial reign on earth, I became a low caste pariah simply because I no longer believed that the Bible teaches that the Second Coming of our Lord would occur at any moment after His ascension, secretly, and before a period of Great Tribulation.

All too frequently, as soon as I would make the slightest mention of the errors of dispensational speculation, I would lose radio program listeners and supporters, never to hear from them again, never to receive a contribution from them again.

I found that while those evangelicals and fundamentalists who have embraced dispensational error are fond of denouncing divisions within the body of Christ, they themselves are the most divisive of all Christians, the most vicious in cutting off those who simply hold to the historic doctrines of the church with regard to the events surrounding the Second Coming of our Lord. Now, in these last years of my ministry, and in these end times of the "last days" of human history, I've got nothing to lose and everything to gain if I can persuade even a few more of God's people to forsake erroneous interpretations of scripture, and to prepare themselves instead for the times of terrible trouble and tribulation that lie ahead.

With this in mind let us continue to list and examine fifteen more truths that I learned about the errors of dispensational interpretation of scripture that I learned from Dr. Jim. (Because of my intense interest in, and on-going studies of this subject, I have, in some instances, lost the distinction between what I learned from Dr. Jim and what I learned for myself. But I will endeavor to place Dr. Jim's teachings earlier in the long list.)

13. "For God hath not appointed us to wrath, but to obtain salvation by our Lord Jesus Christ." (I Thess. 5:9)

This scripture does not teach that God's people are not to experience and endure tribulation, small or great. The Apostle Paul taught "…that we must through much tribulation enter into the kingdom of God." (Acts 14:22) Dispensationalists don't like Acts 14:22 *at all*. It has *saints, tribulation,* and the *Kingdom of God,* all three in it!

Dr. Jim, who had a thorough knowledge of the Greek language of the New Testament pointed out to me the clear distinction made in scripture between *tribulation* (thlipsis) and *wrath (orge)* In only two instances—Romans 2:9 and II Thess. 1:6—is tribulation (thlipsis) mentioned as an act of God against sinners.

In every other instance in the New Testament tribulation is an act of an ungodly world against God's people, which they are repeatedly taught to expect, including *great tribulation,* while wrath is an act of God against, not His own people, but against a wicked world. The wrath of God is never mentioned as being visited by God upon His saints. (see II Chron. 19:2)

Therefore it is clear that to teach that I Thess. 5:9 is an assurance that the church, Christian saints, God's people will not go through the Great Tribulation is another misinterpretation and deception of dispensationalist, pre-tribulation rapture teachers. God's people are never promised that they will escape the world's tribulation, either small or great. How many times must it be repeated in order to clear up the confusion created by the dispensationalists on this point?

14. The salvation and protection that Noah and his family experienced in the ark during the Great Flood 4,500 years ago *is not* a type of the rapture of the church prior to the Great Tribulation.

In the first place, the Great Flood was God's wrath upon a wicked world, not the tribulation of a wicked world inflicted upon God's saints. The tribulation occurred before the rain began to fall. After that it was wrath.

Secondly, Noah and his family never left earth. So their experience cannot possibly typify the snatching away of the church of Jesus Christ to be with Him in glory.

Noah's building of the ark in the midst of a wicked world, followed by the rains and the flood, are a perfect picture of the endurance of the righteous in the face of tribulation and divine deliverance in the midst of God's wrath against the wicked.

That a Christian leader would write an entire book based on the ark-rapture deception is truly shameful, but altogether typical of the lengths to which the dispensationalists and pre-tribulation rapturists will go to support and propagate their unscriptural imaginations.

The Bible is full of instances of persecutions and tribulation directed against God's people, from which there is often no escape, as well as God's wrath directed against a wicked world, from which His people are often protected.

As a matter of fact, Noah's family's salvation from the wrath of God is a biblical prophetic sign of the Great Tribulation and final wrath of God upon a wicked world. Matthew 24:37-41. Luke 17:26-37. Note carefully that those who are "taken," and the carcass that is eaten by the vultures, speak of judgment, not the rapture. Also II Peter 3:5-7. Noah and his family were not "taken" in judgment; they were "left" in deliverance. The pre-tribulation rapturists have got it backwards!

15. Continuing in Matthew 24, the "Olivet Discourse," Dr. Jim exposed the inexcusable misinterpretation and misapplication of those "taken" in the field, at the mill, and in bed. (Matthew 24:40-41 and Luke 17:34-36.)

"Taken" in these scriptures clearly signifies being taken in judgment, not the rapture. Those who did not repent and believe in Noah's day were taken in judgment. Noah and his family were not those who were taken, as a supposed type of the rapture. They were those who were left, spared, saved.

Following these images of judgment, our Lord's disciples asked him, "Where Lord?" He answered that the vultures and buzzards gather wherever the dead carcasses are.

This is anything but a pretty picture of an any-moment secret rapture of the saints. Our Lord is clearly teaching that His coming again, in power and glory, will be a time of the snatching away and cleansing up of the stinking, wicked carcasses of the dead in sin on the great "last day" of resurrection and judgment.

It is indeed shameful that pre-tribulation rapture prophetic teachers would dare to twist scripture in this manner, making the word "taken" mean exactly the opposite from what our Lord clearly intended it to mean.

16. Dispensational teachers speak ominously of the horrors of the Great Tribulation, and assure Christians that God loves them so much He would never permit them to experience such pain and suffering.

In the first place, such a doctrine can nowhere be found in scripture.

Secondly, Foxes' Book of Martyrs and other historic documentation prove that God's people have always been the targets of an ungodly world's fury.

Thirdly, human beings can only endure so much pain, suffering, and tribulation before death comes. Every torture and tribulation that can be invented by depraved men against God's people has already been invented and used. "Great Tribulation" cannot be "great" in the sense of extreme physical suffering.

Fourthly, "great" in "Great Tribulation" points to the worldwide extent of an ungodly world's persecution of the church of our Lord Jesus Christ. There have always—even now—been pockets of intense persecution of God's people. "Great Tribulation," in the context of the final one world government of Antichrist, will be, not a localized, but a worldwide persecution.

And finally, there is a hint of racism and elitism in the pre-tribulation rapture teaching that implies that today's American and Western civilization Christians will be exempt from the Great Tribulation.

For 20 centuries Christian saints from the Roman Empire to Communist China, on every continent in every anti-Christian country, have lost their lives in localized great tribulations.

But this end-times pre-tribulation rapture teaching identifies "God's fortunate few" who are privileged to be Christians in the U.S. and in other mainly white Caucasian civilized nations, who will be spared the exact same fate that their brothers and sisters in the faith met during 20 previous centuries.

It is a gross misinterpretation and misapplication of scripture, and a cruel false hope. We need to be preparing ourselves for the same kind of treatment on a worldwide scale that our Christian brethren have experienced for 2,000 years of church history, instead of hoping to be snatched away before worldwide tribulation begins.

17. There is not one scripture—not one —that teaches that the rapture of the church will be secret or silent.

Yet the *"secret rapture"* is one of the fetishes of the pre-tribulation rapturists and dispensationalists.

As with many dispensational errors, the *"secret rapture"* is diametrically opposed to the plain words of our Lord Jesus, Who Himself will preside over the final resurrection and rapture on the last day. He said, "Wherefore if they shall say unto you...Behold he is in the secret chambers; believe it not." (Matthew 24:26)

Indeed there are many scriptures that teach the very opposite of a "secret," "silent" rapture. In the next verse of scripture, following the one cited above our Lord said, "For as the lightning cometh out of the east, and shineth even unto the west; so shall also the coming of the Son of man be." (Matthew 24:27)

Then, in verse 31, "And he shall send his angels with a great sound of a trumpet, and they shall gather together his elect from the four winds, from one end of heaven to the other."

But since these scriptures do not fit the pre-tribulation rapture dispensationalists scheme of things, they conveniently and deceitfully remove Matthew 24 and 25 from the church age, relegating it to the "tribulation saints" (minus the church). But as I have already pointed out, there will not be two gatherings, two raptures, two resurrections, or two last days. The resurrection, rapture, and judgment that our Lord is talking about in Matthew 24 and 25 is the only one.

Let us no longer be deceived by the pre-tribulation rapture dispensationalists. The great resurrection of the saints of all ages, accompanied by the Second Coming of our Lord Jesus Christ, and followed by the rapture of the Surviving church will be a spectacular, noisy event that will be seen and heard around the world.

Part and parcel of the "secret" error is another error, namely that the rapture of the church will be so secret and silent that it will be like the coming of a "thief in the night." (Thess. 5:2, Matthew 24:43, II Peter 3:10, Rev. 16:15) But they don't tell us that "the thief in the night" metaphor is directed, not at those who are ready, the saints, the church, but at those who are not ready.

The element of surprise is on the part of the ungodly, not the righteous who are eagerly anticipating the return of their Lord. All the pre-tribulation secret rapturists would have to do to be honest in their teaching is to go on to verse 4 of I Thess. chapter 5, "But ye, brethren are not in darkness that that day should overtake you as a thief."

But such honesty is not in their agenda. They know that many of their "students" are uninformed, superficial Christians with ears itching to hear a novel dispensational "truth" so they habitually conceal relevant scripture and twist "inconvenient" scriptures that do not help them build their flimsy house of cards.

18. All three Greek words which denote the Second Coming of our Lord Jesus Christ are used interchangeably to describe that great event, contrary to the musings of the dispensationalists.

In their constant attempt to put every detail of Second Coming truth into their predetermined neat little categories, the dispensationalists and pre-tribulation rapturists have instead put themselves into many big binds.

One such example is their assertion that two of the three Greek words used for our Lord's return denote two different phases of that coming—*parousia* before the Great Tribulation, and *apokalupsis* after the Great Tribulation.

Such error is easy to put over on unsuspecting, eager Bible conference attendees (as I once was myself), but absolutely unsupportable and deceptive.

Believe it or not, pre-tribulation rapturists, apokalupsis (apocalypse, revelation) sometimes occurs in connection with the rapture of the church, while parousia (coming, presence) sometimes occurs in connection with Christ's coming in glory, power, and judgment.

Many proofs of this deception can be found in the New Testament.

Matthew chapter 24 which the dispensationalists say is for the Jewish tribulation saints, begins and ends with *parousia*. Matthew 24:3, 24, 27, 38, and 29.

II Thessalonians 1:8 says that the wicked will be destroyed with the brightness of Christ's *parousia* coming.

In II Peter 3:4 and 12, Peter, describing the coming fiery judgment, uses *parousia* twice.

Not exactly the silent, secret rapture! As far as *apokalupsis* (apocalypse, revelation) is concerned, the word is used by Paul in I Corinthians 1:7, "waiting for the coming of our Lord Jesus Christ," and by Peter in I Peter 1, the "appearing of our Lord Jesus Christ."

In both cases the Second Coming of our Lord is the coming which Paul's and Peter's readers are to look for. *Apokalupsis* (apocalypse) does not connote a secret, silent event.

There is one more New Testament Greek word which denotes the Second Coming of Christ, which exacerbates the dispensationalists' problems. It is *epiphania*, which translated literally is "manifestation."

Paul uses this word five times—I Timothy 6:14, II Timothy 1:10, 4:1, 4:8 and Titus 2:13. In these five instances Paul covers several Second Coming events: Christ's appearance in glory, resurrection and rapture, judgment, and the kingdom.

So we see, dear reader, that the three Greek words that the Holy Spirit used to denote our Lord's Second Coming are used interchangeably with respect to every phase and aspect of that great event on the last day.

19. Another neat but erroneous little gem of dispensational deception is that the "day of Christ" is the day of resurrection and rapture before the Great Tribulation, while the "day of the Lord" is His coming in judgment at the close of the Great Tribulation.

What is the truth of scripture on this point?

In the first place, there is only one last day of Second Coming, resurrection, rapture, and judgment, not two. (See John 6:39, 40, 44, 54, 11:24, and 12:48 and my point 12.)

Frequent references are made to this great "last day" in scripture. "He that hath appointed a day." (Acts 17:31) "The day of wrath and revelation." (Romans 2:5) "The day of visitation." (I Peter 2: 12) "The day of judgment." (II Peter 2:4 and 3:7) "The day of God" (II Peter 3:12) "The day of judgment." (I John 4:17) "The judgment of the great day." (Jude 6) "The great day of his wrath." (Revelation 6:7) "That great day of God almighty." (Revelation 16:14)

There can be no dispute that there is one single day of judgment, which could last as long as 1000 years. "One day is with the Lord as a thousand years." (II Peter 3:8) (It will not be 1007 years as Mr. McGee erroneously and unscripturally asserts.)

But what I want to prove under 19 is that "the day of Christ" and "the day of the Lord" are one and the same. Easy.

A problem for the hairsplitting dispensationalists is, of course, I Corinthians 1:8: "The day of our Lord Jesus Christ." Which is it? The day of Christ? Or the day of the Lord?

The same Corinthian Christians who were anticipating resurrection and rapture (1 Corinthians 15) looked toward the "day of the Lord Jesus." (II Corinthians 1: 14)

"The thief in the night" simile (I Thessalonians 5:2), the pre-tribulation rapturists' mainstay, is found in one of the earliest of Paul's writings, I Thessalonians. The problem for the dispensationalist is that the "thief in the night" simile is linked both with "the day of the Lord" (I Thessalonians 5:2), and the church's meeting "the Lord in the air." (I Thessalonians 4:17)

Always remember, dear reader, that Paul did not put a chapter division between our chapters four and five. He was writing about the same event not two events separated by seven years.

And II Peter 3:10 clearly and simply declares "the day of the Lord will come as a thief in the night," not exactly what the pre-tribulation rapturist evangelists and Bible conference teachers proclaimed in years gone by. The "thief in the night" event, according to the pre-tribulation rapture teachers is supposed to occur seven years before the "day of the Lord" event.

There are other relevant scriptures, but I think I have made the point.

20. The Resurrection of saints is the great end-times theme of both the Old and New Testaments, not the rapture of surviving

saints. (See point number 10)...by man [Jesus Christ] came also the resurrection of the dead...in Christ shall all be made alive...they that are Christ's at his coming." I Corinthians 15:21-23.

The resurrection of the dead is linked with Christ's coming—singular "*coming*," not two comings.

According to the pre-tribulation rapturists, that resurrection will take place...not at His coming...but at an event seven years prior. (See point number 12, only one "last day.")

The pre-tribulation rapturists would have us believe that seven years prior to the *one coming* mentioned in I Corinthians 15:23, the major resurrection and rapture will take place, to be followed by *another* minor resurrection and rapture on *another* last day!

Dear reader, "last" means "last"—only one. The last day of July is the 31st, not the 30th or August 1st.

21. "The resurrection of the dead" is the main theme of the last portion of I Corinthians 15:42-58, not the rapture.

"We shall all be changed." Paul is writing about the resurrection of the dead. The rapture of surviving saints follows the resurrection, of course, as Paul emphasized in another scripture, I Thessalonians 4:17.

22. This great resurrection and rapture event will occur "...at the last trump" (I Corinthians 15:52), not at the next to the last trumpet. It is the same last trumpet mentioned in I Thessalonians 4:16 and Matthew 24:31.

23. These prominent events of the last day and the last trump are in perfect harmony with what we find in Matthew 24, Mark 13, and Luke 21.

God's elect, both the living and the dead, are the object of salvation in these passages, and the wicked are the object of judgment.

The elect are the same elect mentioned throughout the New Testament, not some kind of special, unbiblical category of post-rapture "tribulation saints."

"...but for the elect's sake." (Matthew 24:22 and Mark 13:20)

"...if it were possible they shall deceive the very elect." (Matthew 24:24 and Mark 13:27)

"...and they shall gather together his elect. . ." (Matthew 24:31 and Mark 13:27)

The "elect," following the establishment of Christ's church on earth, are the elect, the only elect, not a new category of elect suddenly appearing after the rapture of the first group of elect. (Please try to figure that out, dear reader.) As I said In Part One of this series, the dispensationalists and pre-tribulation rapturists have so complicated, confused, and convoluted the events of the Second Coming of our Lord Jesus Christ that it is extremely difficult to straighten it all out!!

As far as I'm concerned, the frantic efforts of the pre-tribulation rapturists to make a distinction between the saints before and after a fictitious pre-tribulation rapture is another deliberate deception, pure and simple. There is absolutely no New Testament authority for making such a distinction.

24. Just as in I Corinthians 14, I Thessalonians 4, II Peter 3, and other New Testament scriptures on the doctrine of the Second Coming of our Lord Jesus Christ, His Second Coming will be a spectacular noisy affair. There will be nothing secret about it.

There is not one verse of scripture in the New Testament that says that the Second Coming of our Lord to raise the righteous dead of all ages, to rapture the surviving saints, to judge the world, and to establish His one thousand year reign on earth will be a silent, secret event.

Keep in mind, we absolutely reject the dispensational heresy that the Sermon on the Mount (Matthew chapters 5, 6, and 7), the Olivet Discourse (Matthew chapters 24 and 25, Mark chapter 13, and Luke chapter 21) and other portions of the Gospel account are not for the church in this Age of Grace.

25. The disciples to whom our Lord addressed the Olivet Discourse were among the elect saints, members of His church, and those who established His church on Pentecost. They were commissioned to teach "all things" that our Lord had taught them. "All things" includes the Olivet Discourse, the Sermon on the Mount, and the entire contents of the four Gospel accounts. The dispensationalists' penchant for dividing and cutting and discarding scripture (stemming from an improper interpretation of II Timothy 2:15) to fit their unbiblical notions of which scripture belongs to which era (dispensation) of God's dealings with

mankind, Israel, and the church, is pernicious heresy, and, as such, their false teachings have weakened the church of Jesus Christ in these end times.

The notion that the Olivet Discourse is for the "tribulation saints" to be in force after the rapture of the church, is not supported by one New Testament scripture. It is time for Christ's church to discard these deadly satanic deceptions.

26. The church is addressed and mentioned in the Olivet Discourse. "...but for the elect's sake..." Matthew 24:22 "The elect" in the New Testament always means those who are members of the church and body of our Lord Jesus Christ.

"...if it were possible they shall deceive the very elect." Matthew 24:24 As always during this church age, Christ's elect church are the objects of Satanic deception.

"...they shall gather together his elect from the four winds, from one end of heaven to the other." Matthew 24:31 This is a clear reference to the resurrection and rapture, taught so plainly in I Corinthians 15 and I Thessalonians 4. (Revelation 4:1 has absolutely nothing to do with the resurrection and rapture of saints at the Second Coming of Christ.)

27. Our Lord's warning against the deceptions of false messiahs—Matthew 24:4, 5, 11, 23, 24—is very consistent with other New Testament warnings, such as II Thessalonians 2:9-12 and Revelation 13:13-14. The Great Tribulation will be a time of great deception, against which Christ's church must be on guard constantly.

28. The main characteristic of the Second Coming of our Lord Jesus Christ, the resurrection of the bodies of saints dead in Christ, and the rapture of remaining (surviving) saints is that these events together will be a spectacular noisy manifestation of Divine Power.

These great events to take place at the conclusion of the Great Tribulation will be "as the lightning" (v. 27), like vultures cleaning up dead flesh (v. 28), accompanied by cataclysmic happenings in the sky (v. 29), visible and audible worldwide "with a great sound of a trumpet" (v. 30), "with power and great glory" (v. 30), like Noah's flood (vv. 37-41), and like the calamity of a burglar to unprepared victims (v. 43).

All these characteristics of the Second Coming of our Lord are in perfect harmony with every New Testament scripture on the subject. There is not one word of scripture to support a secret, silent, pre-tribulation resurrection and rapture.

CHAPTER 6

Israel, the Jews, the Church, and the Kingdom of God

29. The parable of the fig tree in Matthew 24, Mark 13, and Luke 21 has absolutely nothing to do with the people or nation of Israel. Our Lord Jesus Christ Himself said that the appearance of the leaves of the fig tree signified the appearance of the some 15 signs that He had just given the disciples.

We have fig trees on the premises of our King's Business and missionary hospitality home headquarters. Every springtime, after all the trees are full of new leaves, and when we think the fig tree is dead, suddenly the leaves appear. Then hot weather is certain.

This, our Lord said plainly, signifies His Second Coming and judgment. When all 15 signs appear in great frequency and intensity, then we can know assuredly that His Second Coming is near.

What authority do Bible teachers have to ignore the divine interpretation offered by the Teacher of the Olivet Discourse, and substitute instead their own "Israel" interpretation?

It is time that we discard every misinterpretation and false hope of the dispensationalists, and prepare ourselves for conflict with him "whose coming is after the working of Satan with all power and signs and lying wonders, and with all deceivableness of unrighteousness in them that perish; because they received not the love of the truth, that they might be saved." II Thessalonians 2:9-10. These words were written by a church member to church members, for the benefit and instruction of all church members till Jesus returns.

30. The thirtieth error and deception of the dispensationalists and pre-tribulation rapturists is the elevation of rebellious unsaved Jews to a high position in the plan of God that is contrary to the whole purpose of the New Testament, and that cannot be found even in the Old Testament scriptures.

The keystone of the arch that holds up the dispensational structure is this shibboleth: "God has earthly promises for His earthly elect, and heavenly promises for His heavenly elect." Such a notion cannot be found anywhere in scripture and does violence to the doctrine of the New Covenant established between God and all mankind (including Israelites and Jews) by the blood of the crucified, buried, and risen Christ.

Why, I have met some Christians who are so enamored and smitten by non-Christian, even anti-Christian Jews that it seems to me that they might prefer to be unsaved Jews instead of saved Gentiles!

The "earthly promises to earthly people/heavenly promises to heavenly people" dichotomy cannot be found anywhere in church history until the 1800s when the Darbyites invented and popularized it. The following are elements of this Darby/Scofield/Lindsey error:

a) Even in this New Testament era God maintains and will keep His "earthly promises" for his "earthly people."

b) Jesus Christ, the Son of God came to this world the first time to fulfill these "earthly promises" to God's "earthly people," namely, a worldwide Jewish Kingdom with the throne in Jerusalem.

c) But His proffered Kingdom and kingship were rejected. Rejected, they were merely postponed until a later date, because God cannot renege on His promises to his "earthly people." (Would these dispensationalist deceivers then say that thousands of first century converted Jews had dealt themselves out of those promises of God to his "earthly people," having become His "heavenly people"?)

d) Although there are no signs to precede the Second Coming of Jesus Christ (just forget I Thessalonians 5 and II Thessalonians 2), He will not return before a massive movement of Jews back to their "promised land" takes place, so that they will be in a position to be the recipients of God's "earthly promises" to them.

e) Christ's church, therefore, in view of (d) above, should look for, hope for, pray for, encourage, and actually participate in this return of Jews to their "promised land," so that His Second Coming can occur, and so that God's "earthly people" can receive their "earthly promises." (How can an event that has no signs to precede it be preceded by such an obvious event?)

f) The great program of God's "earthly promises" for his "earthly people" will resume after a "parenthesis" of 20 centuries, with the "any moment," "secret," "pre-tribulation" disappearance of Christ's church from the world.

g) The target of the terrible persecutions and tribulations to be visited upon the people of the world by world rulers following the disappearance (rapture) of the church will be—not the church of Jesus Christ in opposition to anti-christ as His church has opposed the spirit of anti-christ for 2000 years—but God's "earthly people," unsaved Jews, who are being prepared for the fantastic (root word fantasy) earthly Kingdom promises to be given them when King Jesus comes back (following a seven year hiatus with His church), to take up where He left off when God's "earthly people" rejected His Kingdom and kingship offer nearly 2,000 years ago. Only those Jews who survive the Great Tribulation will be around to realize their long-sought-after earthly Kingdom under their messiah.

(Will there be a second resurrection for those Jewish martyrs who believed and were saved during the Great Tribulation? Will they miss out on the "earthly promise" of the earthly Kingdom?)

Conclusion

I will not waste our valuable time and space to cite the scriptures that Darby/Scofield/Lindsey use to advance these false teachings. It is just all too fantastic (root word, fantasy) to take seriously.

(One of their deceptions, that they consistently avoid confronting, is that most of the people who call themselves Jews today are not the Semitic descendants of Israel, but of the Turkish-Caucasian people of the Khazarian Kingdom of the region between the Black Sea and Caspian Sea, southeast of Ukraine. They migrated into Ukraine and Poland, and eventually to all the nations of Eastern Europe, and finally to Western Europe and the U.S.A. Today they make *aliyah* to Palestine, raise money for their "homeland," and lobby the U.S.

Congress for money for Israel, but they have no ethnic roots whatsoever in Palestine.)

The *biblical* truths are plain and simple. God's promises have always and only been for those, like Abraham, who believed Him and were accounted to be righteous. The patriarchs (Adam through Abraham), the Israelites, the Jews, and gentiles have always and only been saved "by grace through faith." There are no other promises for any others. Jesus came to this world to shed His blood, to die, to be buried, and to rise again the third day in order to accomplish and perfect the way of salvation for lost sinners. He did not come to establish an earthly kingdom for God's "earthly people." Jesus did indeed establish His kingdom and His throne at that time. See Acts chapter 15 and many other such scriptures on the subject of the Kingdom of God. Jesus predicted the time and circumstances of His Second Coming on the last day after a period of Great Tribulation during which His church will be severely persecuted worldwide. His thousand year reign on earth will be but the first "day" (see II Peter 3:8) of eternity. Only His "heavenly people," His "elect saints," His blood-washed blood-bought church will be the recipients of God's "heavenly promises."

The New Testament is clear that our Lord Jesus Christ has broken down the middle wall of partition between God and man and between the various "races" of mankind and that there is now "no difference." How could Christians who are students of the word of God ever embrace the errors and deceptions of the dispensationalists and pre-tribulation rapturists, who say that there is a special variety of humanity that has found special favor in the eyes of God apart from the love and grace of our Lord Jesus Christ? The only hope of Israel is in the Gospel of Jesus Christ.

31. The return of our Lord, the resurrection of saints of all ages, and the rapture of surviving saints, will be a spectacular, noisy event, on a day settled in heaven (not at "any moment"), and to be witnessed by all the people of earth (not secret). These are the simple truths that Christians of all ages believed, until the appearance of dispensational pre-tribulation rapturism.

But in order to "prove" their dispensational and pre-tribulation rapture theories, dispensational teachers must skip over clear scripture to the contrary, and worse, actually conceal contrary scripture from their trusting students.

One of the most notable instances of this kind of deception and error is relative to the first few verses of II Thessalonians. These facts are indisputable:

(1) The Apostle Paul is addressing the saints, the church, and the body of Christ. Verse 4

(2) He reminds them that they are suffering for the "Kingdom of God," at that very time, not at some manifestation of the Kingdom of God in the future. Verse 5

(3) Paul tells these Christian saints to expect the coming of Jesus Christ with His mighty angels. Verse 7

(4) This Second Coming of Christ will be in flaming fire taking vengeance on unbelievers. Verse 8

(5) At His Second Coming, Jesus Christ will commence the punishment and destruction of unbelievers. Verse 9

(6) At His Second Coming Jesus Christ will be glorified and admired by His own.

32. All this described in the first chapter of II Thessalonians is anything but a secret, silent event. Furthermore, it is pure sophistry to claim that although Paul instructed those Christians in clear language to look for these events, that not they, but "tribulation saints" would witness them.

The return of our Lord Jesus Christ to raise the dead, rapture surviving saints, and judge the world will be a spectacular, noisy event, and will be observed and experienced by the whole world.

The second such scripture that denies a silent, secret resurrection of departed saints and rapture of surviving saints is the fourth chapter of I Thessalonians, the very favorite scripture of the pre-tribulation rapturists to prove the silent, secret rapture!

In this well-known scripture Paul made it abundantly clear that the Second Coming of Christ to raise the dead and rapture surviving saints will be accompanied by (1) a divine shout, (2) an angelic voice, and (3) God's very own trumpet. To allege that only God's Old Testament and New Testament saints will see and hear that spectacular event (not a wicked world) is a sophistry and dispensational deception, absolutely unsupported by even one scripture.

The spectacular, public nature of this great event is further described in chapter 5. (Remember, there were no chapter divisions in Paul's letters to the churches.) In this chapter we learn further that the same ones in chapter 4 who "are alive and remain" (4: 17) will witness "sudden destruction" (5:3) likened to the inevitable, unavoidable pain of childbirth. They are further reminded that these spectacular events will not surprise them like the unexpected strike of a thief (5:4).

These events preceding the Second Coming of Christ, the resurrection of the dead, and the rapture of surviving saints will be spectacular, will be seen and heard by all mankind—saints and sinners alike.

Now let's return to II Thessalonians for more proof of the spectacular return, resurrection, and rapture.

In the second chapter of II Thessalonians Paul tells the church at Thessalonica that he is appealing for them to understand on the basis of the Second Coming of Christ (verse 1). He says that this great "day of Christ" (the same as the "day of the Lord" in I Thessalonians 5:2) is not yet near at hand. He says that the "day of Christ"—the same day as the "day of the Lord"—will not take place prior to two important events: an apostasy, and the revelation of "the man of sin," "the son of perdition." The clear implication is that the church of Jesus Christ will be on earth to observe both the apostasy and the revelation of "the man of sin."

To allege that the church will not be a witness to these events, despite the fact that I and II Thessalonians were written to the church, is another sophistry and deception of the dispensationalists.

Another glimpse of the spectacular nature of the Second Coming, which Thessalonian Christians were told to look for, is found in the eighth verse of chapter 2: Antichrist will be consumed with the words of the mouth of Jesus Christ, and destroyed "with the brightness of his coming"—hardly a secret, silent event.

These events surrounding the Second Coming of our Lord Jesus Christ, the resurrection of the dead, and the rapture of surviving saints will be spectacular, and will be seen and heard by all mankind—saints and sinners alike.

32. The various truths and aspects of the Kingdom of God are among the happiest, most encouraging, and most glorious of the entire word of God, and meant to be understood and cherished by the church, the body of Christ. It is also clear from the New Testament scriptures that the Kingdom of God should be proclaimed to unbelievers and taught to believers.

So it never ceases to amaze me (to use a hackneyed old saw) the ease with which dispensational teachers and preachers put over their unbiblical notions about the Kingdom of God on their fawning followers. Any Christian who reads his Bible even occasionally ought to see through their myths, errors, and deceptions.

Before we turn our attention to what the Bible really says about the Kingdom of God, we must list the dispensationalists' bold but erroneous assertions. They assert that:

1. It was always in the plan of God for there always to be a Jewish Kingdom for His chosen people, ruled over by Kings Saul, David, and Solomon, and their successors, and finally, by King Jesus. It could be said that to the dispensationalists this bedrock "doctrine" is the *raison d'etre* for both the Bible and the Messiah.

2. That the principal (only?) purpose for the coming of our Lord Jesus Christ into the world was to reestablish the Jewish Kingdom in all its glory.

3. That Jesus began his public ministry by holding out the hope of an immediate Jewish Kingdom, with Himself sitting on the throne in Jerusalem, and that if the Judeans (Jews) had accepted His offer it would have happened. Really!

4. That the Old Testament "dispensation of law" ended, being replaced by the new "dispensation of grace" when (nobody agrees on exactly "when") the Jews rejected this King and His immediate Kingdom, with the now necessary death, burial, resurrection, ascension, and coming again of the rejected King. In other words, "Plan # 1" failed; our Lord was forced to proceed to "Plan #2."

5. That at some point in their service to their rejected King, the Apostles went into the world, never preaching again the

Gospel of the rejected Kingdom, but only the Gospel of the Grace of God.

6. That they taught that the King could and would return at any moment after His ascension into heaven, secretly, to remove those saved by grace, so that He, the rejected King, could return to resume His original plan to establish His Jewish Kingdom on earth.

7. In addition, we are given to believe that there are different Kingdoms for different New Testament writers, different Kingdoms for different periods of history, and different Kingdoms for different characters marching across the pages of the New Testament. (I haven't got the time or the space to delineate these Kingdom monstrosities.)

Authentic Kingdom Truth

The truth is that all Kingdom citations in the New Testament are interchangeable with each other (Kingdom of God, Kingdom of Heaven, Kingdom of Christ, His Kingdom, etc.)

The truth is that all New Testament characters preached and taught the Kingdom of God from the beginning of their association with the eternal King until the end of their lives on this earth.

The truth is that the Kingdom of God was one of the major themes in the ministry of our Lord Jesus Christ *at all times*—in Galilee, later in Judea, and finally as He steadfastly set his face to go to Jerusalem." (Luke 9:51)

His Kingdom and Kingship were prominent topics during the night and following day of His crucifixion. Even the thief on the cross prayed to be remembered in His Kingdom.

After the resurrection our Lord appeared to His apostles "by the space of forty days, and speaking the things concerning the Kingdom of God." (Acts 1:3)

Preaching and teaching the Kingdom of God were not temporary or intermittent themes of the eternal King, the Son of God.

The Kingdom of God in the Book of the Acts of the Apostles

The eternal King taught His disciples "things pertaining to the Kingdom of God." (Acts 1:3)

Philip preached the "things concerning the Kingdom of God." (Acts 8: 12)

Paul and Barnabas exhorted the believers in Lystra, Iconium, and Antioch "to continue in the faith, and that we must through much tribulation enter into the Kingdom of God." (Acts 14:22)

In Ephesus Paul taught in the synagogue, "persuading the things concerning the Kingdom of God." (Acts 19:8)

Paul spent his last days in Rome "preaching the Kingdom of God, and teaching those things which concern the Lord Jesus Christ." (Acts 28:31)

How could anyone teach that there is any dispensation to be found in the Acts of the Apostles in which the truths of the Kingdom of God were not in the plan, purpose, and will of God?

The Kingdom of God in the Pauline Epistles

Was the Apostle Paul a good dispensationalist? Did he refrain from teaching and preaching the Kingdom of God in favor of the Gospel of the Grace of God? His letters to the churches speak for themselves.

I have already cited Paul's ministry to the saints of Iconium, Lystra, Derbe, Ephesus, and Rome.

In one of his earliest letters, to the Thessalonians, he taught, "...walk worthy of God, who hath called you unto his Kingdom and glory." (I Thessalonians 2:12) And later, to the same Thessalonian Christians, "...be counted worthy of the Kingdom of God, for which ye also suffer." (II Thessalonians 1:5)

To the Galatians, Ephesians, and Colossians: "...they which do such things shall not inherit the Kingdom of God." "...hath any inheritance in the Kingdom of Christ and of God." "...fellow workers unto the Kingdom of God." (Galatians 5:21, Ephesians 5:5, and Colossians 4:11.)

Paul wrote to the Corinthian Christians, "For the Kingdom of God is not in word but in power." And "...the unrighteous shall not inherit the Kingdom of God...nor extortioners shall inherit the kingdom of God." And "...flesh and blood cannot inherit the Kingdom of God." (I Corinthians 4:20, 6:9-10, 15:50)

Before he made his last journey, to Rome, Paul wrote to the Roman Christians, "For the kingdom of God is not meat and drink; but righteousness, and peace...and joy in the Holy Ghost." (Romans 14:17)

In both of his letters to Timothy, Paul mentioned the "eternal King" and His kingdom. (I Timothy 1:17, II Timothy 4:1) he concluded the first letter with the glorious words! "...our Lord Jesus Christ...the blessed and only Potentate, the King of kings, and Lord of lords." (I Timothy 6:14, 15)

And finally, one of the most inspiring and empowering expressions of the truth of the Kingdom of God in the Bible is this scripture from Hebrews (which I believe to have been written by the Apostle Paul): "Wherefore we receiving a kingdom which cannot be moved, let us have grace, whereby we may serve God acceptably with reverence and godly fear." (Hebrews 12:28)

The Kingdom of God According to the King Himself

There are approximately 100 verses of scripture in the four Gospel accounts Matthew, Mark, Luke, and John—that present a truth concerning the Kingdom of God. Most of these are from the lips of the King Himself.

Upon Whom could we rely more to help us understand the Kingdom of God than the King Himself?

Could the Son of God have been devoting so much time and attention to a transitory, less-than-top-priority doctrine?

Could He possibly have been excluding any of the truths of the Kingdom of God when He commissioned His disciples, "...teaching them to observe all thing's whatsoever I have commanded you"? (Matthew 28:20)

As I have already pointed out in different words, our Lord's teaching concerning the Kingdom of God extended from the beginning of His ministry..."Except a man be born again he cannot see the kingdom of God." (John 3:3)...and never was suspended for any reason whatsoever.

Moreover, neither the reality of the eternal Kingship of Christ nor the existence of His eternal Kingdom depended in any way whatsoever on their acceptance or rejection by the multitudes. (It is a great error of the dispensationalists to teach that since the King and His kingdom were rejected, they were no longer a reality, but temporarily suspended to be reinstated at a later date.)

More Sophistries

Another wise sounding error of the dispensationalists, and absolutely without foundation is the sophistry that there are different kingdoms (Kingdom of God, Kingdom of Heaven, Kingdom of Christ., etc.), and that these different kingdoms are presented by different writers at different times in different ways for different purposes, etc., etc., *ad nauseam.*

A reasonable examination of the 100 kingdom citations in the four Gospels clears up all these gems of confusion and more, produced by the dispensationalists for 175 years. Here, in my way of thinking, are the highlights.

There are six instances in which Matthew, Mark, and Luke record the same teaching of our Lord, and in which Matthew records "Kingdom of Heaven," while Mark and Luke record "Kingdom of God."

This means that since they are reporting the same teaching or event, no difference in meaning can be assumed.

These six are (1) Matthew 4:17 and Mark 1:15, (2) Matthew 5:3 and Luke 6:20, (3) Matthew 11:11 and Luke 7:28, (4) Matthew 13:11, Mark 4:11, and Luke 8:10, (5) Matthew 13:31 and Mark 4:30, and (6) Matthew 19:23, Mark 10:23, and Luke 18:24. In a seventh instance Matthew records "his kingdom"—Matthew 16:28, Mark 9:1, and Luke 9:27.

(I think the explanation for these differences in wording in the exact same teachings and events is that although our Lord Himself used "Kingdom of God" and "Kingdom of Heaven" interchangeably,

Matthew decided on "Kingdom of Heaven," while Mark and Luke decided on "Kingdom of God." In cases where only one of the four records an event or teaching, Matthew usually uses "Kingdom of Heaven.")

But to the consternation of the dispensationalists, in at least three instances Matthew reports the words of our Lord to be the "Kingdom of God." (19:24, 21:31, and 21:43)

And in eight instances Matthew records simply "the Kingdom," "his Kingdom," or "the Kingdom of their father," proving further that Matthew joined the other Gospel writers in their proclamation of one *and only one* Kingdom.

So it is clear that the dispensationalists simply are not able to divide the Kingdom into many pieces as they are prone to do with all scripture.

Concluding Thoughts

Just as the dispensationalists have set law against grace, they have tried to set the Gospel of the Kingdom of God against the Gospel of the Kingdom of Heaven, and both against the Gospel of the Grace of God.

Neither is exclusive of the other. Law vs. Grace, and the Kingdom vs. the Church are not biblical distinctions. All should be believed, taught, and proclaimed.

(I was accused of being a "legalist" in Japan for beginning the proclamation of the Gospel with the Law of God. The Kingdom of God occupied a major place in my teaching and preaching. Both of these "strategies" help account for the immediate and lasting fruitfulness of our ten years there.)

Law reveals the holy nature of God. Grace reveals His love for sinners and plan of redemption and reconciliation.

The Kingdom reveals the universal authority of God. Grace and the Church of Jesus Christ constitute one sphere within His eternal Kingdom.

Kingdom teachings get our attention. What boy or girl, what adults, are not fascinated with the idea of kings and queens, pomp and circumstance, majesty and authority?

The Kingdom of God speaks to us of the absolute authority of a holy God Who is never wrong about anything in the administration of His Kingdom.

The Kingdom of God speaks to us of a sphere of authority embracing the entire universe as well as planet earth, together with the saints of God of all ages, including His Church in this Age of Grace. None of earth's tyrants will escape the absolute and eternal authority of His Kingdom.

The Kingdom of God speaks to us of a King...a perfect King...the "King of kings and Lord of lords," our Lord and Saviour Jesus Christ. He demands and deserves our total admiration and loyalty.

Too long have the dispensationalists intimidated us with their Kingdom vs. Church dichotomy, making us believe that we can be good evangelicals and fundamentalists only if we believe their "myths, errors, and deceptions" concerning the Kingdom, and making us believe that we are less than evangelical and fundamental believers if we dare preach the "Good News of the Kingdom of God," as our Lord and His disciples did.

Let us throw off their oppressive propaganda and brainwashing once and for all.

Peter, James, and John

What do the three disciples closest to the eternal King say to us about this important and very serious doctrine?

"For so an entrance shall be ministered unto you abundantly into the everlasting Kingdom of our Lord and Savior Jesus Christ." (II Peter 1: 11)

"Hath not God chosen the poor of this world rich in faith, and heirs of the Kingdom which he hath promised to them that love him?" (James 2:5)

"I John, who also am your brother, and companion in tribulation, and in the Kingdom and patience of Jesus Christ..." (Revelation 1:9)

CHAPTER 7

Conditional Covenants and Promises,
Not Unconditional

*G*ermane *to the topics of Israel, the Jews, and the church, which we focused on in the preceding chapter, is the topic of* covenants *and* promises. *The most important covenant and promise in all of scripture is that of salvation of fallen man "by grace through faith." This covenant and promise was in effect in the Old Testament dispensation, and is now in effect in this New Testament dispensation. It is set forth clearly in the 3rd chapter of Galatians, a passage of scripture that Israel-first dispensationalists rarely read or teach. This covenant and promise is simply that lost sinners of all of earth's inhabitants who have the same kind of faith that Abraham had are the children of God. "There is no difference." Read it for yourself. (Abraham was a Semite, a Hebrew, and a Chaldean. He was neither an Israelite nor Jew.)*

It is most important to remember, in dealing with the covenants and promises of scripture, that an "everlasting covenant" is not necessarily an "unconditional covenant." The covenant and promises in Exodus 19:5-6, for example, is an Old Testament promise of blessing and salvation, an eternal and everlasting promise by a God of love and grace, but it is a conditional promise because it contains the words "if" and "then." (Read Deuteronomy chapter 28, one of the longest chapters in the Bible, for many more "ifs" and "thens"...another chapter of the Bible never heard about from the Israel-first dispensationalists.) And, as far as Exodus 19:5-6 is concerned, we must conclude that it was a spiritual "heavenly promise for a heavenly people," not an "earthly promise for an earthly people" (to use the Israel-first dispensationalists' own terminology), because it is repeated almost verbatim in I Peter 2:9.

Let us now consider, alongside the deceptions of Mssrs. Darby, Scofield, Lindsey, McGee, LaHaye, et al., some simple, basic truths about the covenants and promises of scripture.

Another area of Bible study and interpretation in which the dispensationalists are flagrantly in error and cunningly (deliberately?) deceptive is that of the covenants between God and man. Three general examples of this error and deception will serve to establish this point before we go on to specific scriptures.

First, our Christian Bible makes a distinction between the Old Covenant (Testament) and the New Covenant (Testament), teaching us that the Old has been replaced by the New. But the dispensationalists deny this basic Christian doctrine when they insist that there are Old Testament covenants that continue on into the New Testament era.

Second, the dispensationalists find the "Jew," the "children of Israel," and the twentieth century nation "Israel" in certain Old Testament covenants and promises, when the truth is that the "Jew" is never mentioned, and today's Israel is in no way a fulfillment of any Old Testament covenant, promise, or prophecy of any kind.

Third, the dispensationalists are fond of citing certain "unconditional" covenants between God and man, when the truth is that there is not one unconditional covenant in all of scripture. The truth is, further, that God has never promised His blessings, unconditionally, to those who rebel against His word, who disparage His law, who blaspheme His Name, who deny His Son Jesus Christ, and who persecute His people. (This just happens to be the condition, of most so-called Jews in the world today.)

Monumental Ignorance or "Cunningly Devised Fables?"

I do not hesitate to say that the birth of dispensationalism in the 1700s, and the rise of dispensationalism in the 1800s, and the world-wide popularization of dispensationalism in the 1900s are the work of Satan. But to what extent fallible human beings, including Christians, knew that they were formulating "cunningly devised fables" I do not know.

At the very least we can say that Darby, MacIntosh, Scofield, Lindsey and many others seem to delight in elevating and exalting rebellious Israel over and above the sanctified, blood-washed church of our Lord Jesus Christ. In his notes, Scofield frequently extols the wonderful accomplishments of "Israel," while disparaging the work of the church.

Beyond that, and more likely, there is the possibility that nineteenth century British and American dispensationalists were so enamored of the program of the Eastern European Jewish "Zionists" that they, mesmerized and deceived, developed a system of Bible interpretation that harmonized with Zionism. (Although the word "Zionism" has absolutely no connection with the beautiful biblical word "Zion," or "Sion" it *appears* to denote something good. However, it has turned out to be one of the most evil movements in human history, literally stealing Palestine from the Palestinians, with the approval of England, the U.S. and evangelical dispensationalists worldwide! Some have even speculated that C.I. Scofield was able to sell his "Scofield Bible" to the British publishing house, *Oxford,* because it would help advance the cause of the Eastern European "Zionists!")

Scofield or Scripture?

Let's try to sort out this mishmash of novel, heretical interpretations of the word of God, as space permits in this installment of "Errors and Deceptions."

We will begin with what is perhaps the most flagrant dispensationalist error and deception of all—their interpretation of Genesis 12:1-3.

The Promises to Abraham

The correct Holy Spirit inspired interpretation of this passage is found in the third chapter of Galatians. These are the key truths: Abraham was saved by grace through faith. His seed was Jesus Christ, through Whom all the families of the earth would be blessed. All who, by grace through faith, are members of the body of Christ (Abraham's seed) claim Abraham as their father. Thus this promise or covenant has been completely fulfilled. There is no further fulfillment of Genesis 12:1-3 for which we should look.

But the dispensationalists, totally ignoring Paul's exposition of the covenant of Genesis 12:1-3, (1) link Abraham with Israelites and Jews, (2) create a new category of covenants and promises "earthly promises for earthly people," (3) and spin the myth that Christians and Christian nations who "bless" anti-Christian Jews will be blessed by God. (Note: America's era of greatest decline has been the very years that we have financed and kowtowed to anti-Christian Israel!)

The Davidic Kingdom Covenant

Dispensationalists completely thwart God's new Covenant (New Testament) by bringing His Son, our Lord Jesus Christ down to the level of a secular, earthly kingship. This kingship, according to Scofield, was hoped for in the first century, but is now postponed till much later.

Again, God's revealed fulfillment of these covenants and promises in such scriptures as Acts 2:25-36 and Acts 15:13-17 are trashed in favor of the dispensationalists' wild imaginations.

Dear reader, our Lord Jesus Christ is now sitting on the eternal throne of David. He is the eternal King ruling over an eternal kingdom.

Unconditional Covenants

Plainly and simply, there are no unconditional covenants and promises in scripture. We should be convinced of this every time we read the little word "if," especially in the Old Testament.

It follows that all of God's Old Testament promises and covenants have been fulfilled for the faithful and obedient remnant, as well as denied the unfaithful, disobedient, rebellious multitude.

In this New Testament dispensation God's elect, the body of His Son our Lord Jesus Christ, today's "remnant," His "heavenly people," will in no way whatsoever compete with or run parallel to imaginary promises and covenants with an imaginary "earthly people," which have been continued over from the Old Testament dispensation, and which have bestowed upon ungodly Jews and ungodly Israel a prominence absolutely unwarranted either by scripture or common sense.

CHAPTER 8

Christian, Not Judeo Christian

*F*riends, to me, one of the most disgusting and repugnant combinations of words in the English language is "Judeo-Christian," as in: "Our Judeo-Christian heritage" or, "The Judeo-Christian foundations of the United States of America."

The two words, or concepts, or religions that form "Judeo-Christian" are self contradictory and mutually exclusive. The two together create confusion, a fiction, an illusion, a non-existent monstrosity.

"Judeo-", of course, comes first from "Judah"—one of the sons of Jacob. Then from "Judea"—Jerusalem and environs. And finally from "Judaism"—a religion that had its beginnings during the Babylonian captivity.

The simple fact is that the religion of Judaism had nothing whatsoever to do with the establishment of this once Christian nation. So why do the preachers and politicians let this despicable phrase, "Judeo-Christian" flow from their mouths with such ease and frequency?

Well, I confess, I have some idea about the answer to that question because at one time I myself was using the nice-sounding term, "Judeo-Christian." My naive reasoning was that since America was founded on the Bible—both the Old and New Testaments—that it was truthful to describe our history and heritage as "Judeo-Christian."

I not only revealed my ignorance of the religion of Judaism, its history and scriptures, I was willing to divide the credit for the glorious beginnings of this nation between Divine Truth and human error.

Now it is my desire to correct all that, and to seek to persuade others who have accepted the same error that I *accepted to abandon it as I did. You have never heard me use this obnoxious term "Judeo-Christian" on "The King's Business" radio program, and you never will, except as I am using it now.*

In this message we will examine what's behind this strange, pervasive development in language under five headings: the obsequious motivations for it, the misguided thinking in it, the dishonorable compromise associated with it, the unsound theology underlying it, and the flawed history behind it...our "Judeo-Christian heritage."

The Obsequious Motivations in "Judeo-Christian"

The first and foremost motivation for using the term "Judeo-Christian" that comes to mind is to curry favor with the two percent Jewish population of the U. S . There are six million intelligent, well educated, influential, and prosperous Jewish citizens in this country, who vote and who contribute vast sums of money to various causes and charities, even to churches. They also hold positions of great power in large organizations, and can dispense huge amounts of either grief or blessing as they decide.

Motivation?

Politicians want the votes and the money, and, of course, the election and reelection victories. Radio and TV preachers want the approval and contributions of their pro-Israel fanatic Christian listeners, and to be left alone by the Jews. Above all, neither the pols nor the Revs want to be accused of being anti-Semites. So a nice "Judeo-Christian heritage" thrown in a speech or sermon now and then goes a long way.

The politicians have learned that even one vote on Capitol Hill contrary to Israel's best interests can mean defeat at the next election, and the preachers have learned that the best way to get a good job with a nice salary is to comfort Israel-first Scofield dispensational evangelical Christians with the cheerful, uplifting phrase, "Judeo-Christian heritage." The radio and TV preachers covet the generous contributions that come from their Israel-first audiences. And many of these preachers reassure us that America's Judeo-

Christian heritage is a factor in the return of Jews to Israel and the return of Christ to earth.

Yes, it all sounds so good, so pleasant—the "Judeo-Christian history and heritage of the United States of America." It is so full of discernment and understanding and good will. But this use of "Judeo-Christian" is fraught with the evils of fawning, kowtowing, and ultimately cowering in the presence of the enemies of Christian America.

And while we are on the subject of what motivates our "Judeo-Christian heritage" radio and TV preachers and their generous contributors, we mustn't forget the famous television preacher who is fond of telling the world, in the most sanctimonious tone of voice, "Gawd has blessed America because America has blessed the Jew."

"Jerry, have you been asleep these past fifty years of America's sin and decline while supporting Israel?"

And then there are those millions of superficial Christians who hear and see these radio and television preachers, who think it is just dandy that we can show our appreciation to "God's Chosen People" for helping us establish and build this nation, so they use the pleasant words, "Judeo-Christian heritage."

Oh yes, before we leave this point, let's not forget that it was Christians who invented such an odious term. The "Judeo" faction of "Judeo-Christian" is too smart for that. But maybe they did invent it after all. Let's ask the debonair Rabbi Yechiel Ekstein, who established and built a multi million dollar organization that takes money from obsequious Christians to give to Christ denying Jews in Israel. And the rabbi is laughing all the way to the bank.

The Misguided Thinking in "Judeo-Christian"

When questioned about their use of the term "Judeo-Christian," our evangelical and fundamentalist friends readily admit that they are merely trying to convey the idea that the Old Testament was written in Hebrew for the Jews…the "Judeo" part…while the New Testament was written in Greek for the Christians…the "Christian" part. Therefore they say since America was founded on both the

Old and New Testaments they should refer to our "Judeo-Christian" heritage."

America's beginning was, they say, "Judeo-Christian."

But such a dichotomy is baseless, needless, useless, inane, misguided and misleading. The first glaring reality is that most Jews have little regard for either Moses and his law, or the prophets and their preachments. Bible believing Christians, including the Founding Fathers, have a tenfold greater faith in and respect for the Old Testament than do Jews.

The second glaring reality is that there were only a handful of Talmudic (not Old Testament) Jews around during the days, weeks, months, and years of the establishment of this Christian nation, so even if some had been Old Testament believing Jews, what influence could they possibly have had?

Thirdly, Scofield-influenced evangelicals and fundamentalists who are fond of the phrase "Judeo-Christian" are simply ignorant of the relationship between the Old and New Testaments.

A fundamental tenet of the Christian faith is that the Old and New Testaments are a harmonious unity, setting forth the holiness, justice, love, and saving grace of Jehovah God for people of all ages. God's love and saving grace were extended to both Israel and the Gentile nations through the Hebrew Old Testament scriptures. In the first century the writers and readers of the Greek New Testament were likewise both Israelites and Gentiles. During the transition years from Old to New Testaments (the events reported and recorded in Matthew, Mark, Luke, John, and the Acts), the Hebrew Old Testament were the *only* scriptures available and in use. During those days *only* those descendants of Jacob who *correctly* understood the Hebrew Old Testament believed in Jesus and built His church.

God said in His word "There is no difference" several times. Why should we make a difference now, with "Judeo-Christian"? America's history and heritage are Christian only; only Christian.

The Old and New Testaments are not two sets of scriptures for two groups of people—Jews and Christians—upon which America was established. America's founding, heritage, and history are Christian, not Judeo-Christian, the outcome of the Christian scriptures, Genesis 1:1 through Revelation 22:21.

This kind of straight thinking will help us abandon the inane term, "Judeo-Christian."

The Dishonorable Compromise in "Judeo-Christian"

If by mouthing "Judeo-Christian" America's sycophantic politicians and fawning preachers intend to advance the notion that America was established on two religions and their two scriptures, they are guilty of gross ignorance or contemptible compromise, or both.

Worse, if they are implying the popular notion that Judaism gave birth to Christianity, or that Judaism and Christianity are basically the same, they need to find and take a good course in World Religions 101.

"Judeo" is derived from "Judaism," which has its scriptures, the Talmud. "Christian" has unmistakable religious connotations, and is derived from the Bible, both the Old and New Testaments. Anyone who is knowingly willing to put Judaism and its Talmud on a par with Christianity and its Bible when characterizing America's beginnings and heritage is guilty of blatant compromise, and denial of the uniqueness of Christ, to say nothing of heaping insult on America.

Judaism is not the religion of the Old Testament. It is a religion concocted first by rebellious priests and scribes during the Babylonian captivity. They discarded much of the Torah (Old Testament law), killed God's prophets, and instituted their own religious dogmas and ceremonies. Pagan occult teaching and practices became a major feature of Judaism. When added to and written down through the centuries, the scriptures of Judaism became known as the Talmud.

The Talmud is pure rebellion against Jehovah God. It explains how a man can violate a three year-old girl and not be punished; how a priest can hire the services of a prostitute in the temple and not be punished; and how a man can break all his agreements and vows without consequences—"Kol Nidre." It will also tell you about the private life of Jehovah.

Dr. Jacob Gartenhaus, beloved Hebrew Christian evangelist and scholar, whom I heard preach and teach in the 1930s, describes the

Talmud in these ways: "Ridiculous tales," "ludicrous speculation," "obscene jokes," "obnoxious desires," "strange words," "absurdities," "pure nonsense," and "one of the world's strangest and most confused books."

Friends, to link these "religious" writings and the religion they represent, Judaism, with the history and heritage of the United States of America, is a blatant violation of God's warning against compromise with evil found in Ephesians 5:11 "Have no fellowship with the unfruitful works of darkness, but rather reprove them."

Dear listener, is Judaism's Talmud a part of America's heritage? Did the Pilgrims and Puritans consult Judaism's Talmud when they formulated their early governments? Did the writers of the Declaration of Independence, Constitution, and the Bill of Rights derive any of their convictions from the scriptures of Judaism? No, of course not. America's history and heritage are not Judeo-Christian. Then let's stop using such a compromising manner of speech.

Now, does Talmudic Judaism have any role in our 20th and 21st centuries "Judeo-Christian ethic?" It shouldn't. But the answer to that question is unfortunately and ironically, "Yes."

By uttering these oh-so-pleasing words, "Judeo-Christian," our preachers and politicians don't realize the extent to which they are admitting and abetting the betrayal of America.

The historical fact is that a long line of Judeo-Talmudic rabbis, philosophers, psychologists, sociologists, educators, lawyers, judges, economists, and other intellectuals, have very nearly succeeded in turning this nation away from its Old Testament and New Testament Christian heritage. Indeed, the roots of the situational ethics, moral relativism, spiritual rebellion, and Humanism that are destroying America today descend in to the pages of the Talmud. Our once Bible-based law schools, courts, and judges are now advocates of what I call "But Law." "God says, but..." "Moses says, but..." "The Bible says, but..." "The Constitution says, but..."

When America's religious heritage is examined objectively and honestly, it must be characterized as a Christian heritage, not a compromised Judeo-Christian heritage or any other kind of hyphenated Christian heritage.

Unsound Theology in "Judeo-Christian"

"Judeo-Christian" connotes two diametrically opposed religious systems.

Judaism does not recognize the divine inspiration and authority of the Old Testament, much less the New. Christianity recognizes the divine inspiration and authority of both.

Our Lord Jesus Christ had to make this point plain during the years of His ministry: "And ye have not his word abiding in you; for whom he hath sent, him ye believe not." "For had ye believed Moses, ye would have believed me; for he wrote of me. But if ye believe not his writings, how shall ye believe my words?" John 5:38 and 46-47)

Judaism denies that our Lord Jesus is the Messiah, the Anointed One, and Jehovah God. Christianity recognizes Him as Christ, the Messiah, the Anointed One, Jehovah God.

Jesus, Paul, and all the Apostles continually struggled against Judaism—the dogma that the "traditions of the elders" superseded the word of God. "Thus have ye made the commandment of God of none effect by your tradition. Ye hypocrites, well did Isaiah prophesy of you saying, this people draweth nigh unto me with their mouth, and honoureth me with their lips; but their heart is far from me. But in vain they do worship me, teaching for doctrines the commandments of men." (Matthew 15:6-9) "Ye stiffnecked and uncircumcised in heart and ears, ye do always resist the Holy Ghost: as your fathers did, so do ye. Which of the prophets have not your fathers persecuted? and they have slain them which shewed before of the coming of the Just One; of whom ye have been now the betrayers and murderers; who have received the law by the disposition of angels, and have not kept it." (Acts 7:51-53)

Christ and His Apostles condemned the very thing today's fawning politicians and preachers speak of approvingly: Judaistic Christianity. Don't today's preachers who talk about America's Judeo-Christian heritage understand the inspired words of the Bible?

Perhaps a listing of ten of the most fundamental keys to an understanding of the uniformity of the Old and New Testaments will serve to solve the problem of "Judeo Christian" usage, and enable us never again to use the phrase, "America's Judeo-Christian heritage." This nation was not founded upon two religious systems, simply because:

- The Old Testament pointed to the events of the New Testament.
- The central Character of the Old Testament is the promised Messiah, Who is revealed in the New Testament.
- Saving faith in the Old Testament was the same as saving faith in the New Testament, that is, the same kind of faith that father Abraham had.
- Saving faith in the Old Testament predated the appearance of the Israelites, Moses, the Law, and the religion of the Jews.
- God's saving grace in the Old Testament extended to the same people as His saving grace in the New Testament, that is, to the believing "remnant" of any and all racial backgrounds.
- The descendants of Abraham, Isaac, and Jacob of New Testament times who understood the old Testament Scriptures readily believed in Jesus Christ. These understanding, believing Jews included Zecharias and Elisabeth, Joseph and Mary, the shepherds, Simeon and Anna, John the Baptist, and any others.
- The descendants of Abraham, Isaac, and Jacob of New Testament times who did not understand the Old Testament Scriptures disbelieved and opposed our Lord Jesus Christ, John the Baptist, and the Apostles.
- Our Lord's major antagonists during His ministry on earth were those who did not believe the Old Testament Scriptures, but who had substituted their own traditions instead. (These oral traditions of the elders were the beginnings of the Talmud, the foundation of modern Judaism.)
- Among the Apostle Paul's major antagonists were those who did not see the true spiritual implications of the Old Testament Scriptures upon the events of the first century. Inspired by the Holy Spirit, he based his writings entirely upon the Old Testament.

- INDEED, THE ONLY SCRIPTURES USED BY THE FIRST CHRISTIAN CHURCHES WERE THE OLD TESTAMENT SCRIPTURES. THOSE FIRST CHRISTIANS, THE TRUE SPIRITUAL DESCENDANTS OF ABRAHAM, USED THE OLD TESTAMENT JUST LIKE THE NEW TESTAMENT IS USED TODAY, PROBABLY MORE SO, AS PEOPLE "SEARCHED THE SCRIPTURES."

The Flawed History behind "Judeo-Christian"

The first groups of people who explored and settled America were Christians. They were Bible believers. They believed both the Old Testament and New Testament scriptures to be the inerrant and authoritative word of God. (They brought the Geneva Bible of 1599 with them, not the King James Version of 1611. I call the Geneva Bible the "Passover Bible." See Acts 12:4 of both versions.)

They established their homes, their schools, their communities, their cities, colonies, states, and their nation upon the whole counsel of God—not part of it, not additions to it, not a perversion of it.

They recognized Jesus Christ as the King of kings and Lord of lords, and as the One to Whose honor and glory this new nation should be dedicated. They were not Christ-rejectors or Christ-deniers.

They are the ones who had the faith and the vision and the courage to establish this nation. They are the ones who shed their blood, gave their lives, and who made other incredible sacrifices, proving the genuineness and divine origin of their faith.

The others, with their false faiths, their false religions, and their false scriptures, such as the Talmud of Judaism, came later.

Therefore, anyone who was not, or is not the kind of Christian described above has no claim whatsoever to any participation in the founding heritage of the United States of America, because America's is a Christian heritage.

If we look at America's beginnings through the hearts and minds of its founders we find that they had in mind leaving us who came along later with a "Christian heritage," not a "Judeo-Christian heritage."

Those who drafted and approved the Constitution of the New England Confederation wrote, "Whereas we all came into these parts of America with one and the same end and aim, namely to advance the kingdom of our Lord Jesus Christ and to enjoy the Liberties of the Gospel in purity with peace."

Patrick Henry would have been a good president. Instead he was the friend and advisor to all our early presidents, and *pro bono* defender of many Virginia Baptist preachers against public beatings and imprisonment by Virginia's established church, the Church of England, *in the years before and after the Declaration of Independence.* He wrote: It cannot be emphasized too strongly or too often that this great nation was founded, not by religionists, but by Christians, not on religions but on the Gospel of Jesus Christ! For this very reason peoples of other faiths [such as Judaism] have been afforded asylum, prosperity, and freedom of worship here." (Author's paraphrase: "...and the right to undermine and destroy what we have created.")

John Adams, our second President, from 1797 to 1801 uttered these and similar words on many occasions: "Our Constitution was made only for a moral and religious people. It is wholly inadequate to the government of any other." (Note: When the Founding Fathers used the word "religion," and "religious" they were referring to the Christian faith.)

James Madison, who was President from 1809 to 1817 wrote this and many similar truths before, during, and after his presidency: "Religion [Christianity] is the basis and foundation of government." And, "We have staked the whole future of American civilization...upon the capacity of each and all of us to govern ourselves, to sustain ourselves according to the Ten Commandments of God."

Supreme Court Justice Joseph Story, appointed to the Supreme Court by President Madison, wrote in one of his decisions, "The real objective of the First Amendment was not to countenance, much less advance, Mohammedanism, or Judaism, or infidelity, by prostrating Christianity...Christianity ought to receive encouragement by the state...Any attempt to level all religious, and to make it a matter of state policy to hold all in utter indifference would have created universal disapprobation, if not universal indignation." (Justice Story mentioned Judaism by name!)

John Jay, together with Patrick Henry, was a Christian firebrand of the Revolution. In 1789 he was appointed by President George Washington to be Chief Justice of the Supreme Court, and served six years. Then he was elected to be Governor of New York, and later the first president of the American Bible Society. On one occasion he said clearly and unequivocally, "Providence has given to our people the choice of their rulers, and it is the duty, as well as the privilege and interest of our Christian nation to select and prefer Christians for their rulers." On his deathbed in 1829 Jay's last words were, "Unto Him Who is the Author and Giver of all good, I render sincere and humble thanks for His merciful and unmerited blessings, and especially for our redemption and salvation by His beloved Son." (What chance would John Jay have to be confirmed as Chief Justice of the Supreme Court today? Moreover, as I have said many times on "The King's Business" radio program through the years: If James Madison, Alexander Hamilton, and John Jay could have looked down the corridors of time into the future, and seen the tyranny that their Federal Government was to become, they never would have written their "Federalist Papers.")

Around the same time in the history of our country, in the first half of the 19th century, the great statesman and orator Daniel Webster declared that America began "...with the very first foundations laid under the divine light of the Christian religion...let us not forget the religious [Christian] character of our origin."

In 1892 Supreme Court Justice David Brewer wrote for the majority, "These, and many other matters which might be noticed, add a volume of unofficial declarations to the mass of organic utterances that this is a Christian nation." He said in a speech at Harvard in 1905: "This republic is classified among the Christian nations of the world. It was so formally declared by the Supreme Court of the United States...we constantly speak of this Republic as a Christian nation—in fact, as the leading Christian nation of the world."

President Woodrow Wilson declared, "America was born a Christian nation. America was born to exemplify that devotion to the elements of righteousness which are derived from the revelation of Holy Scripture."

Friends, in these very few quotations out of the past we are confronted with the reality of the presence of the Christian faith in our American history and heritage, and only once with the reality of the faith of Judaism, and that in a negative context. I wish today's preachers and politicians could bring themselves to speaking after the manner of America's founders. We are a nation with a Christian history and heritage. Anyone who speaks of our Judeo-Christian history is simply ignorant of America's history.

Have We Morphed into a Judeo-Christian America?

Ironically and tragically, while America's history and heritage are not Judeo-Christian, present day America can certainly be characterized as Judeo-Christian. Our culture, our morals, our law, our civilization, even our Christian religion, have been Judaized. Yes, it is disheartening to have to admit that our popular evangelical cult of dispensationalism has helped advance the emergence of our new Judeo-Christian America.

The Judaization of America is one of the arenas in which we must "fight the good fight of faith," and display militant Christianity, "...pulling down strong holds...bringing into captivity every thought to the obedience of Christ."

Since changing my mind about this very serious matter, I have become so convinced of (and thankful for) the great Christian heritage of our beloved nation that I have come to resent the phrase "Judeo-Christian heritage." You have never heard me use this term on "The King's Business" radio program, and you never will.

And I will continue to use this radio ministry to point out this error to our well-meaning politicians here in Washington and to our patriotic preachers all over the country, as God enables me to do so. There is absolutely no justification—historical, biblical, or otherwise to share the credit for the glorious beginnings of America with a false system.

When God places His stamp of approval upon a nation, and blesses it, and empowers it to accomplish His purposes, it doesn't mean that that nation will remain pleasing and acceptable in His sight. Just as a small amount of poison will pollute a river, unbelievers, agnostics, atheists, and evil men of all persuasions can turn a nation away from the divine purposes that were present in its beginnings.

So it has been with our once Christian U.S.A., and it just may be too late to turn it around. The Marxists, the socialists, the atheists, the Judaists, the Humanists, the moral relativists, and the evolutionists have tried to shove all that remains of our Christian heritage to backstage. Christians, showing great patience for these devourers, assuring them of their First Amendment rights, and mouthing such words as "Judeo-Christian" have provided them a great opportunity for success.

But the temporary triumph of evil over good, and error over truth, is never a reason for God's people to abandon a total, uncompromising attack for truth and right. We need to remind the nation and the world of the *Christian* heritage of America, and fight the same battle our forefathers fought for Christ and His Word.

The United States of America was brought into existence by God through the faith, vision, and sacrifices of *Christian* people in order to accomplish certain *Christian* objectives among its own people, as well as among the people of the world.

America has strayed far away from her Christian heritage, but that heritage is still worth fighting for, without compromise or accommodation.

CHAPTER 9

The Crucifixion and Burial on Wednesday, Not Friday

*T*he next two chapters set forth the indisputable truth of the Wednesday betrayal, trial, crucifixion, and burial of our Lord Jesus Christ, and the truth of the conspiratorial efforts of Nicodemus and Joseph to give the world the greatest proof of His resurrection.

As far as the Wednesday crucifixion of our Lord Jesus Christ is concerned...yes, the crucifixion and burial were on Wednesday, not Friday...does this upset you? Well, it did me too when I was first confronted with such a possibility, after 30 years of Good Friday celebration.

But I wasn't devastated, as most of us are when our beliefs, traditions, customs, and favorite holidays are challenged.

For, as you must understand, I was born with a question mark on my forehead, doubting, challenging, and suspecting almost everything, a true skeptic.

I never doubted the inspired words of Almighty God, even on such difficult doctrines as creation, the virgin birth of our Lord, His miracles, His vicarious atonement, His resurrection, His Second Coming, etc.

But I did have trouble with dogmas that are not clearly set forth in scripture, such as Christmas celebration, the pre-tribulation rapture, the role of Israel in the Second Coming, and the Friday crucifixion and burial of our Lord, as well as a few others.

Of course, I have run in to those who have advised such a doubting and negative soul as myself, "Why not just grit your teeth, bite your tongue, swallow hard, take a deep breath, and just accept all these dogmas you're having trouble with, and that have been accepted without question by zillions of

Christians for millions of years?" (Author: numbers greatly exaggerated)

Well, on the other hand, maybe there is a place for such folks as I in the world. And that brings me back to the Wednesday crucifixion and burial of our Lord Jesus Christ.

It is very simple, but difficult to explain; as you will see when you read the Bible study I am featuring in this radio broadcast. When the Holy Spirit first struck me with the "three days and three nights" of Jonah and Matthew, my skeptical head said to my skeptical self, "How then can we say that our Lord Jesus Christ was crucified and buried on Friday? 36 hours in the tomb, or 72?"

Another question surfaced many years later. "Does the Bible say that Jesus arose on Sunday morning at sunrise, or only that the tomb was found empty on Sunday at sunrise?" A good question. And a good question with a good answer. Now I will relate briefly some of the history of my discovery of the truth of the Wednesday crucifixion and burial.

I enjoyed a pretty good acquaintance with fellow B.J.U. graduates, the Grubes of Louisiana.

Henry sent me some of his research and writings on the subject. It was sound and convincing but not complete. I knew that there were some pieces of the puzzle to be found in Scripture that would complete the picture.

Many years later I read a quotation by one of the greatest and most revered Baptist scholars, Lee R. Scarborough, in favor of the Wednesday crucifixion and burial. Jim McKeever of Oregon published a study placing the crucifixion and burial on Thursday. And there were others...all close, but none complete and "on the mark."

Continuing to seek the truth of scripture on the question, I suddenly discovered the answer in two very simple, straightforward statements of chronology found in the Gospel accounts.

John 12:1 and Matthew 26:2 place the Passover indisputably on a Thursday (sundown Wednesday till sundown Thursday), and therefore the crucifixion and burial of our Lord the day before (sundown Tuesday till sundown Wednesday)!

Nicodemus and Joseph,
Three Days and Three Nights

I tell you the truth; I lie not. I never heard a sermon or lecture, or read a writing on the subject of Nicodemus' and Joseph of Arimathea's conspiracy to prove the truth (or prove the potential deception) of the resurrection of our Lord Jesus Christ.

Yet, there are several corroborating incidents and circumstantial evidences clearly set forth in scripture that establish such a sincere, conscientious, holy conspiracy on the part of these two "secret" disciples of our Lord.

Why did I never hear or read an exposition of this biblical truth?

Perhaps I'm to blame. Perhaps I overlooked an exposition of this biblical truth because I am not a well-read scholar. Perhaps it is because I do not move in the circles of seminary professors, college presidents, TV personalities or Christian celebrities, where such things are discussed.

Or could it be that the fact that two Sanhedrin members collaborated to prove the resurrection is just not important?

To some, perhaps it is not. After all, the great Apostle Paul proved the resurrection of our Lord adequately in the 15th chapter of I Corinthians, didn't he? Why bother with any additional proof?

Yes, with these arguments I am trying to highlight the careless manner in which we have overlooked the Spirit-led scheme of Nicodemus and Joseph.

As I stated at the beginning of this chapter, I did not discover this truth, with all of its intrigue, twists and turns, and excitement from any teacher or preacher. God revealed these things to me from His word over a period of many years.

How did all this come about?

As a missionary to the Japanese following World War II, I emphasized the very difficult and incredible doctrine of the resurrection of our Lord Jesus Christ after His death on the cross for our sins (Despite the advice of a famous evangelist to preach only the cross and the shed blood. Perhaps this could explain the enduring and flourishing work of Dale Crowley Jr. in Japan for over 50 years.)

I searched the New Testament scriptures for every over-looked or neglected word or incident in connection with the resurrection in order to convince my hearers of Jesus' death, burial, and resurrection.

Of course, I made clear the role of Joseph and Nicodemus in the burial of our Lord. But I overlooked their conspiratorial scheme as members of the Sanhedrin—consummate insiders.

The Holy Spirit did not see fit to bring it all together for me, entrusting the details of this historical verity until the 1970s, when I wrote a preliminary paper on the subject. (To this day I have not recovered that early writing...a satanic attack to obscure a vital truth? Yes!)

But as I anguished over the matter the Holy Spirit recalled to my memory every detail and more, so that now I am sending out these two great truths—the Wednesday crucifixion and burial, and the crucial, indispensable work of Nicodemus and Joseph to establish the fact of the resurrection of our Lord, with all confidence and boldness in these radio broadcasts.

THE WEDNESDAY CRUCIFIXION AND BURIAL OF OUR LORD JESUS CHRIST

The scripture which holds the key for determining the day of the week on which our Lord was betrayed, crucified, and buried is John 12:1:

> **Then Jesus six days before the Passover**
> **came to Bethany, where**
> **Lazarus was which had been dead,**
> **whom he raised from the dead.**

Taken together with John 19:31, the information contained in John 12:1 makes the Wednesday crucifixion and burial irrefutable: The Jews therefore, because it was the preparation, that the bodies should not remain upon the cross on the Sabbath day, (for that day was an high day), besought Pilate that their legs might be broken, and that they might be taken away.

John 19:31 makes two chronological facts clear:
1. **That the crucifixion and burial of our Lord was on the Day of Preparation.**
2. **That the Day of Preparation preceded a high Sabbath day (not the ordinary seventh day Sabbath).**

Therefore, since the Passover of John 12:1 was six days from Friday afternoon, then the Day of Preparation preceding the Passover of John 19:31 would be five days from that Friday afternoon (Nisan 9), or Wednesday Nisan 14.

If the day of our Lord's crucifixion were Friday, then the number in John 12:1 would have to be eight, not six.

The journey to Bethany was on Friday before the Sabbath began at sundown. Jesus observed the Sabbath—sundown Friday till sundown Saturday—in the home of Mary, Martha, and Lazarus.

On the first day of the week He journeyed to Jerusalem for His triumphal entry as the promised Messiah. (Matthew 21, Mark 11, Luke 19:29-44, and John 12:12-19)

Six Days between Nisan 9 and Nisan 15

Therefore it is clear that if the journey to Bethany occurred on Friday afternoon, two days before the triumphal entry into Jerusalem, and six days before the Passover on Nisan 15, then

Passover occurred on Thursday that year, and the crucifixion and burial of our Lord occurred on Wednesday, the Day of Preparation before the Passover Sabbath.

Let us clarify the chronology immediately in this study:

Journey to Bethany Seventh Day Sabbath Begins	Friday	Nisan 9
Seventh Day Sabbath	Saturday	Nisan 10
Triumphal Entry into Jerusalem	Sunday	Nisan 11
Teaching, Cleansing of the Temple	Monday	Nisan 12
Teaching, Olivet Discourse	Tuesday	Nisan 13
Last Supper, Betrayal, Arrest, Trial, Crucifixion, Burial	Wednesday	Nisan 14 (Sundown Tuesday till Sundown Wednesday)
In the Tomb	Thursday	Nisan 15 (Passover Sabbath)
	Friday	Nisan 16 (Unleavened Bread Sabbath)
	Saturday	Nisan 17 (Seventh Day Sabbath)
Resurrection after Sundown Saturday	Sunday	Nisan 18 First Day of the Week

WHAT DIFFERENCE DOES IT MAKE?

Now I agree with those who say, "'I don't care on what day of the week our Lord Jesus Christ was crucified and buried. The important truth is that He died for our sins, was buried, and rose from the dead for our salvation."

But I would hope that the same people would agree with me that if it can be proved from both the Old and New Testaments that our Lord was crucified and buried on Wednesday—not Friday—then we should accept Wednesday to be the day.

I can think of three reasons why knowing the truth about the day of our Lord's crucifixion and burial are important to us as Bible believers and Christians.

First, the Wednesday crucifixion and burial helps us understand the events of the Passion Week better. For example, we ought to be able to account for the events of every day of this momentous week, instead of coming to the conclusion that there were two "silent days" (Wednesday and Thursday) about which we are told that we can know nothing from scripture.

I was taught the two "'silent days" theory and I believed my teachers. The great Bible scholar and seminary professor A.T. Robertson advanced the two "silent days" theory in his monumental work, A Harmony of the Gospels. On pages 188 and 189 he skips over these two days, and explains himself with an unprovable note. This demonstrates how even the most devout and erudite Bible teachers can be wrong.

Second, we should always seek to rid ourselves of unbiblical interpretations and traditions, even those advanced by fellow Christians and Christian religions.

Third, the Wednesday crucifixion and burial of our Lord removes all doubt about His prophetic words recorded in Matthew 12:40: "For as Jonas (Jonah) was three days and three nights in the whale's belly; so shall the Son of man be three days and three nights in the heart of the earth."

We utterly reject the sophistry expressed by Robertson that since the Hebrew calendar reckoned daily time from night to day (sundown to sundown) we therefore can't take the words of our Lord literally. Furthermore, New Testament Greek scholars assure us that the phrase "on the third day," found several times in the New Testament can also mean "after three complete days."

REASONS FOR AND SOURCES OF THE ERROR OF THE FRIDAY CRUCIFIXION AND BURIAL ("Good Friday")

Normal people will ask, "How is it possible that the whole world would accept the wrong day for the crucifixion and burial of our Lord?" This section will explain how it happened.

1. **The first reason for the misunderstanding: The Sabbath day mentioned in John 19:31 was not the seventh day Sabbath. The seventh day Sabbath was not a "high day."**

"The Jews therefore, because it was the preparation, that the bodies should not remain upon the cross on the Sabbath day, (for that Sabbath day was a high day), besought Pilate that their legs might be broken, that they might be taken away."

Thus this scripture is not only responsible for the erroneous tradition of a Friday crucifixion and burial; it holds the key, together with John 12:1 ("six days before the Passover") to determining the true day.

The "Sabbath day" mentioned in John 19:31 was not the seventh day Sabbath (Saturday), as anyone might readily surmise, but instead the Passover Sabbath. The seventh day Sabbath was neither a "high day" in the Jewish calendar, nor was it ever preceded by a day of "preparation." That could only be the Passover Sabbath, which fell on different days of the week from year to year.

The 12th chapter of Exodus sets forth the origin of the selection of the lamb on the 10th of Nisan, the sacrifice of the lamb and the preparation and eating of unleavened bread on the 14th of Nisan, and the Passover event and departure from Egypt on the 15th of Nisan. Also mentioned is the preparation and eating of unleavened bread from the 14th till the 21st of Nisan, with special mention of the preparation and eating of unleavened bread on the 16th of Nisan, the day following Passover.

The 23rd chapter of Leviticus sets forth various laws relative to the observance of these and other Sabbath days.

I repeat, the "day of preparation" and "Sabbath" mentioned in John 19:31 are the two days Nisan 14 and 15, regardless of which day of the week they fall on.

2. **The second reason for the misunderstanding: Ignorance about Old Testament law regarding various Sabbaths.**

This area of misunderstanding is commonplace among Christians. We simply believe that the "Sabbath" means Saturday, or , and no other feast, festival, or day of the week.

But eight feast days established by Old Testament law were Sabbaths, or days of rest. (See Leviticus 23) Three of the eight were "High days"—Passover, Pentecost, and Tabernacles.

As we have already emphasized, and must repeat, the Passover "high day" Sabbath was preceded by a day of preparation, and followed by the Feast of Unleavened Bread Sabbath (not a "high day").

Every year, therefore; there were three important days celebrated in connection with Passover:

Day of Preparation-Nisan 14
Passover Sabbath—Nisan 15 (full moon)
Unleavened Bread Sabbath-Nisan 16

Nisan 14, the Day of Preparation, was also considered a part of the Feast of Unleavened Bread, which lasted seven days. See Matthew 26:17, Mark 4:12, and Luke 22:7. However, it seems that only "the third and seventh days of the feast of Unleavened Bread, Nisan 16 and 21 were counted as Sabbath days.

3. **The third reason for the misunderstanding: Overlooking key scriptures that provide chronological clues to the events of the week which began with the Triumphal Entry into Jerusalem, the so called "Palm Sunday."**

John 12:1—Jesus traveled to Bethany six days before the Passover on Nisan 15.

Matthew 26:1-2 and Mark 14:1-2—"Two days before Passover, spoken by our Lord on Tuesday afternoon following His "Olivet Discourse."

4. **The fourth reason for the misunderstanding: "The two silent days" myth.**

There is absolutely no evidence that two days intervened between Matthew 26:16 and 17, between Mark 14:11 and 12, and between Luke 22:6 and 7.

To put 48 silent hours between these contiguous scriptures is like putting seven years between "that blessed hope and the glorious appearing" of Titus 2:13. This sort of Bible interpretation and teaching does violence to the scripture for the sole purpose of forcing the historical account of the inspired word of God into a preconceived, pre-set false tradition. (See pages 188-189 of A Harmony of the Gospels by A.T. Robertson.)

5. **The fifth reason for the misunderstanding: Misunderstanding concerning the occurrence and sequence of Sabbath days in connection with Passover celebration.**

The Sabbath mentioned in John 19:31, we repeat, was not the seventh day Sabbath. It was the "high" holy day, the Passover Sabbath.

We all know from our own experience with the calendar that the dates of the month fall on different days of the week from year to year.

For this reason there are seven possible combinations of the three Sabbath days (Passover, Unleavened Bread, and the weekly seventh day) that could occur during a Passover week. Those combinations are:

1. Sunday, Monday, and Saturday
2. Monday, Tuesday and Saturday
3. Tuesday, Wednesday, and Saturday
4. Wednesday, Thursday, and Saturday
5. Thursday, Friday, and Saturday .
6. Friday, Saturday-Saturday (the Feast of Unleavened Bread Sabbath and the seventh day Sabbath falling on the same day)
7. Saturday-Saturday, and Sunday (the Passover Sabbath and the seventh day Sabbath falling on the same day)

THE FIFTH ON THE LIST IS THE SEQUENCE OF SABBATHS THAT OCCURRED DURING THE PASSION WEEK RECORDED IN THE GOSPEL ACCOUNTS.

The sixth on the list is the sequence of Sabbaths that is traditionally observed by Christians everywhere, with the Passover and seventh day Sabbaths falling on the same day.

Therefore, when scripture says, in John 19:31, that everyone had to hurry to remove the body of our Lord from the cross and bury it before sundown *on the day of preparation before the Sabbath*, it means that it was late afternoon on Wednesday, just before the beginning of the Passover Sabbath, the 15th of Nisan which was from sundown *Wednesday* till sundown Thursday that year.

6. The sixth reason for the misunderstanding: The difficulty of the night-day method of reckoning a 24-hour day (instead of day-night).

This is a minor point, but it does have some relevance. It simply causes confusion to us whose days begin at 12 midnight to understand events that take place on days that are measured from sundown to sundown. The day of preparation before the Passover Sabbath, and which included the last supper, arrest, trial, crucifixion and burial of our Lord was Nisan 14, which began at sundown Tuesday and ended at sundown Wednesday.

7. The seventh reason for the misunderstanding: The events that took place after sundown Saturday.

The Bible does not say that our Lord rose from the dead on Sunday morning, but that His followers found the tomb empty on Sunday morning. ("Early on the first day of the week" could be anytime after sundown Saturday.)

The portion of the first day of the week from sundown Saturday till sunrise Sunday is counted by just about everyone to be the third day of the three-day burial. The truth is that our Lord rose from the dead immediately after sundown Saturday on the first day of the week, He exited the tomb without the stone being rolled away. The Roman soldiers were guarding an empty tomb all night long!

QUESTION AND ANSWER TIME

Now that we have examined both scripture and tradition, identifying both the source of truths and errors concerning the death, burial, and resurrection of our Lord, let us ask and answer some important questions.

We all know the value of posing questions and finding answers in the pursuit of knowledge. We will ask and answer the questions in a chronological manner, beginning with the pre-Sabbath day journey to Bethany from Jericho.

Question 1. When did our Lord make the journey from Jericho to Bethany?

Answer: It was on Friday afternoon before sundown, on the 9th day of Nisan, two days before His Triumphal Entry into Jerusalem, and six days before Passover. According to Old Testament law, the travel had to be completed before the seventh day Sabbath began at sundown Friday.

(There seems to have been another Bethany, more often known as Bethabara, on the east bank of the Jordan near Jericho where John baptized.)

Question 2. Where did He spend the seventh day Sabbath prior to the Triumphal Entry into Jerusalem and Passion Week?

Answer: With His friends and followers, Mary, Martha, and Lazarus in Bethany. (This visit to Bethany is a different occasion from the visit four days later when there was a feast and anointing at the home of Simon the leper, immediately before the Last Supper and betrayal in Jerusalem.)

This was the 10th of Nisan, the day on which the Jews were selecting the Passover lamb.

Question 3. The Triumphal Entry into Jerusalem happened on the first day of the week, Sunday, but what was the date on the Jewish calendar?

Answer: The 11th of Nisan, from sundown Saturday till sundown Sunday.

Question 4. What were the main events of Monday, the 12th of Nisan?

Answer: The cursing of the fig tree, the cleansing of the temple, and the profound teachings of John 12:20-50.

Question 5. What were the main events of Tuesday, the 13th of Nisan (Monday sundown till Tuesday sundown)?

Answer: The night spent in Bethany, the withered fig tree observed, controversies with the Pharisees and Sadducees in the temple, severe denunciation of the scribes and Pharisees (Matthew 23), the widow's two mites, and the Olivet Discourse on the Mount of Olives.

Question 6. Are there two missing days in the Passion Week—Tuesday evening till Thursday evening—in the accounts of the Gospel writers, or is everyday, Sunday through Sunday, accounted for?

Answer: There are not two missing days. Everyday is accounted for.

Question 7. Were there other Sabbath (rest) days besides the seventh day Sabbath?

Answer: Yes, for example, the Passover Sabbath.

Question 8. Was the Passover Sabbath always preceded by the Day of Preparation (which was also the first day of the Feast of Unleavened Bread)?

Answer: Yes. But the first day of the Feast of Unleavened Bread was not a Sabbath day.

Question 9. According to the Old Testament calendar, what were the dates of the preparation for the Passover Sabbath and the Passover Sabbath itself?

Answer: The Day of Preparation for the Passover booth was Nisan 14 (the night and day before the full moon). The Passover Sabbath was Nisan 15, the night and day of the full moon.

Question 10. Was the Passover Sabbath followed by another Sabbath day?

Answer: Yes, the Feast of Unleavened Bread, Nisan 16. Nisan 16 was the third day of the Feast of Unleavened Bread, Nisan 14 being the first day of the Feast of Unleavened Bread.

Question 11. Did three Sabbath days ever occur in succession to one another?

Answer: Yes. During the Passion Week the Passover Sabbath, the Feast of Unleavened Bread Sabbath, and the seventh day Sabbath fell in succession—Nisan 15, 16, and 17—sundown Wednesday till sundown Saturday.

Question 12. Did Nisan 14, 15, and 16 fall on the same days of the week every year?

Answer: No.

Question 13. Was the seventh day Sabbath, which was observed every week on the seventh day, preceded by a day of preparation?

Answer: No.

Question 14. On what day of the Passion Week did the Passover Sabbath fall?

Answer: On Thursday (sundown Wednesday till sundown Thursday).

Question 15. Was Jesus in the tomb 36 hours from sundown Friday till sunrise Sunday, or 72 hours from sundown Wednesday till sundown Saturday?

Answer: He was in the tomb three days and three nights, from sundown Wednesday till sundown Saturday—three Sabbath days.

Question 16. Were the Israelites permitted to do any work or travel more than a short distance on a Sabbath day?

Answer: No.

Question 17. If the Passover Sabbath had fallen Saturday (sundown Friday till sundown Saturday), could our Lord's followers have made the journey to the tomb and performed the duties that they intended to perform?

Answer: No. Because if the Passover Sabbath had fallen on Saturday (sundown Friday till sundown Saturday) that year, the following day, Sunday, would have been the third day of the Feast of Unleavened Bread, a Sabbath, and that would have prohibited them from making such a journey and performing such duties.

Having examined all the evidence for the Wednesday crucifixion and burial, we will now go to a graphic depiction of the events of the ten day period of time from Friday Nisan 9 till Sunday Nisan 18. (See table, next page.)

Sundown Thursday		Sundown Friday		Sundown Saturday		Sundown Sunday		Sundown Monday		Sundown Tuesday
	Friday Nisan 9		Saturday Nisan 10		Sunday Nisan 11		Monday Nisan 12		Tuesday Nisan 13	
	Preaching and Teaching in Jericho Journey to Bethany 6 Days Before Passover		Seventh Day Sabbath		Triumphal Entry into Jerusalem		Cursing of the Fig Tree Cleansing of the Temple		Observing the Cursed Fig Tree Many Disputes Many Teachings Olivet Discourse At the Home of Simon the Leper	

The vertical lines on the table represent sundown and the beginning

	Sundown Tuesday	Sundown Wednesday	Sundown Thursday	Sundown Friday	Sundown Saturday	Sundown Sunday
	Wednesday Nisan 14	**Thursday Nisan 15**	**Friday Nisan 16**	**Saturday Nisan 17**	**Sunday Nisan 18**	
	Day of Preparation for Passover	Passover Sabbath	Feast of Unleavened Bread Sabbath	Seventh Day Sabbath	Resurrection After Sundown Saturday	
	Last Supper					
	Pray at Gethsemane				Angel Rolls Away Stone	
	Betrayal				Guards Fall Down as Dead	
	Trial				Women Visit Empty Tomb	
	Crucifixion				Guards Bribed	
	Burial				Jesus Appears to the Eleven	

of a new day according to the Jewish calendar.

THE BLESSED NARRATIVE

It is with reverence and thanksgiving that we conclude this study by narrating the travels, events, teachings, sufferings, crucifixion, burial, and resurrection of our Lord from Friday Nisan 9 until Sunday Nisan 18.

Our narrative will be an overview, not in great detail, but based on an authoritative compilation of the events of those ten days from the four Gospels that can be found in the helps section of many Bible. We will use our names for the days of the week in order to avoid confusion, relying on the phrases "before sundown" and "after sundown" to indicate the ending and beginning of the days according to the Jewish calendar.

From Jericho to Bethany

In the morning and afternoon of Friday Nisan 9 our Lord crossed the Jordan River into Jericho, healed blind Bartimaeus and his friends, called Zacchaeus, and was entertained in his home. It was there that the famous words of salvation were declared, For the Son of man is come to seek and to save that which was lost." (Luke 19:10)

Jesus knew that He was on His way to Jerusalem for the last time, so he left Jericho with enough time to arrive in Bethany before sundown Friday, the beginning of the seventh day Sabbath. Bethany was nearly two miles east of Jerusalem and Jericho was about 15 miles northeast of Jerusalem.

John noted that Jesus and His disciples arrived in Bethany six days before Passover. (It was only a few days or weeks earlier that Jesus had raised Lazarus from the dead at Bethany. See John chapter 11.)

The Sabbath in Bethany

Our Lord spent the Sabbath, Nisan 10 in Bethany, with nothing recorded of his activities on that day. Surely He must have remembered that the Law of Moses required the Paschal lamb to be selected on Nisan 10. He was indeed ''The lamb of God that taketh away the sin of the world" (John 1:29), and He may have realized that appointment by God the Father on that very special seventh day Sabbath. (Even though He was acclaimed King on the following day, He knew that He was going to Calvary.)

The Triumphal Entry into Jerusalem

On Sunday morning, Nisan 11, Jesus and His disciples left Bethany for the nearly two mile journey to Jerusalem. When they reached the Mount of Olives He instructed His disciples to find the "colt the foal of an ass" on which He rode into Jerusalem.

Both Matthew and John record that this was the fulfillment of Zechariah 9:9 in which Jesus the Messiah is to be received as King. This is very important because it is not as the dispensationalists say, that Jesus was received and then rejected as King, thus postponing His Jewish kingdom until a later date. Jesus' Kingship was recognized on that day by the multitudes, and that Kingship has never been changed. He is the "King eternal" (I Tim. 1:17).

Jesus ended the event with a short disputation with the Pharisees, and returned to Bethany for the evening.

Sunday after sundown was the beginning of the second day of the week.

Return to Jerusalem

On the way to Jerusalem on Monday morning our Lord cursed the barren fig tree. In Jerusalem he cleansed the temple for the second time (see John 2:13-22). Later in the day the Greek worshippers came to Jesus with their inquiry about Him.

He returned to Bethany again that evening. Monday after sundown was the beginning of the third day of the week.

Return to Jerusalem

On the way to Jerusalem on Tuesday morning our Lord and His disciples observed the withered fig tree, and He gave them a lesson on faith and prayer.

This day, Tuesday Nisan 13 was one of the busiest, and surely one of the most tiring in the life of our Lord. It led directly into the events of Nisan 14, the Day of Preparation which began at sundown, and on which our Lord was crucified, without any sleep or rest after a grueling day.

The events in Jerusalem included a confrontation with members of the Sanhedrin concerning His authority, clever questions from the Pharisees, Herodians, and Sadducees intended to ensnare Him, His most severe denunciation of the scribes and Pharisees, and His commendation of the poor widow's gift.

On the way back to Bethany in the afternoon Jesus stopped at the Mount of Olives with His disciples, where He gave them a long teaching on future events, which we know as the Olivet Discourse. This discourse occupies a large portion of scripture—Matthew chapters 24 and 25, Mark chapter 13, and Luke chapter 21.

The first few verses of Matthew 26, Mark 14, and Luke 22 contain ominous words about the plans of the Sanhedrin (the high priest and the chief priests) to kill our Lord. Both Matthew, and Mark put the time at "two days" before Passover, and Matthew says that Jesus' observation to His disciples came at the conclusion of the Olivet Discourse: "And it came to pass, when Jesus had finished all these sayings, He said unto his disciples, Ye know that after two days is the feast of the Passover, and the Son of man is betrayed to be crucified." (Matthew 26:1-2)

"Two days" from Tuesday Nisan 13 is Thursday Nisan 15, Passover, by which time our crucified Saviour is spending His first day in the tomb.

When Jesus and the disciples arrived back in Bethany they found that dinner was waiting for them at the house of Simon the leper. Also present were Mary, Martha and Lazarus. Mary anointed Jesus' head and feet with expensive perfume, which prompted complaints from Judas and other disciples. Jesus rebuked them.

Immediately after that rebuke Judas left Simon's house, returned to Jerusalem, and bargained with the chief priests for his betrayal of Jesus.

> Two Silent Days?
>   Here is where A.T. Robertson and multitudes of Bible scholars and teachers put their "two silent days," clearly and solely in order to make the biblical narrative fit the Good Friday crucifixion tradition.

But the scriptures do no such thing. Matthew 26:16 is followed by Matthew 26:17, Mark 14:11 is followed by Mark 14:12, and Luke 22:6 is followed by Luke 22:7.

Passover Meal Eaten One Day Early

By the time the anointing and dinner at Simon's had concluded, it was sundown, and Nisan 14, the first day of the Feast of Unleavened Bread which is also the Day of Preparation preceding the Passover Sabbath, had begun.

Apparently our Lord had informed His disciples that they would celebrate the Passover meal one day early on Nisan 14 instead of Nisan 15. This has been the subject of much discussion and controversy, but the explanation is a simple one. If our Lord is to endure the sufferings of the betrayal, the trial, and the cross on the Day of Preparation so that He could be buried before the Passover Sabbath begins at sundown Nisan 15, according to the Mosaic Law, then He had to eat the Passover meal before the Passover Sabbath began. (Thousands were eating the Passover meal during His first hours in the tomb.)

Return to Jerusalem after Sundown Tuesday

It was now Nisan 14, the Day of Preparation for the Passover Sabbath, the day that the Paschal lamb was slain, the day the unleavened bread was baked for the journey out of Egypt after midnight Nisan 15, the day that all preparations were made for the escape out of Egypt on the night of the full moon, Nisan 15.

It was no accident, or coincidence in the Divine Plan that Jesus Christ, the Lamb of God Whose blood was shed, was slain on Nisan

14, at the same time that Israelites everywhere were killing their Paschal lambs.

So Jesus had to eat the bread and drink the cup of the Last Supper early on Nisan 14, sometime after sundown. He sent His disciples to make preparation for the simple commemorative meal.

Before that last meal together our Lord washed the feet of the disciples, identified Judas as His betrayer, and urged His disciples to be loyal.

Following the institution of the Lord's Supper memorial Jesus had many things to say to His disciples. It appears from scripture that He continued teaching them and praying for them on the way to the garden known as Gethsemane, located in the valley between Jerusalem and the Mount of Olives. Several hours of Nisan 14 had already transpired when, in Gethsemane He sweat drops of blood in prayer to the Father.

It was near midnight when Judas, knowing one of Jesus' favorite places for prayer, led a band of soldiers to Gethsemane and betrayed our Lord into the hands of the chief priests and Pharisees.

During the early morning hours of Nisan 14 (Wednesday), there was a hearing before Annas, a former high priest, and then a trial before Annas' son-in-law Caiaphas the high priest. Peter denied His Lord in the courtyard of the high priest, and the cock crew.

At daybreak Wednesday morning, still Nisan 14, the Day of Preparation for the Passover Sabbath, our Lord was condemned by the Sanhedrin.

Judas committed suicide.

Then Jesus went before Pilate for an official government condemnation. Pilate sent our Lord to Herod Antipas, who then sent Him back to Pilate. Pilate ceded to the demands of the Sanhedrin, condemning Jesus to death on the cross.

By 9 a.m. on the morning of Wednesday, Nisan 14, our Lord was on Golgotha's cross (Mark 15:25—the third hour of morning, or 9 a.m.).

There was darkness between noon and 3 p.m. Our Lord died at 3 p.m. His death was accompanied by an earthquake, resurrected saints, and the tearing of the veil of the temple from the top to the bottom.

A Roman soldier said, "Truly this was the Son of God."

There were only three more hours left in the day, the Day of Preparation before the Passover Sabbath. (See the key scripture, John 19:31.) Jesus the Messiah had to be buried before sundown when the high and holy feast day Passover would begin.

During those three hours two men, both no doubt members of the Sanhedrin, insiders, requested from Pilate the body of our Lord for burial. Joseph and Nicodemus prepared the body for burial, accomplishing everything according to the law, before sundown. (The next morning the Sanhedrin, of which Joseph of Arimathea and Nicodemus were members, requested a contingent of Roman soldiers to guard the tomb to prevent Jesus' disciples from stealing the body. Ask for our message on the most astonishing event of scripture, how two Jewish insiders proved the resurrection of our Lord Jesus Christ beyond any shadow of a doubt.)

Our Lord in Joseph's Tomb Three Sabbath Days

That year three Sabbath days fell one after the other—Nisan 15, 16, and 17—Wednesday sundown until Saturday sundown. During those three Sabbath days, according to Jewish law, no one could visit a tomb to perform any of the remembrances or rituals that were customary. In the case of the burial of our Lord it would have been very difficult to do anything with the presence of the Roman guard.

The Resurrection after Sundown Saturday

By the time the women arrived at the tomb while it was still dark on Sunday morning, several momentous events had already taken place.

Our Lord Jesus Christ had risen from the dead, sometime after the beginning of Nisan 18, after sundown Saturday. During the night there was an earthquake; an angel of the Lord appeared like lightning and rolled away the stone. The Roman guard fell to the ground unconscious.

When the women arrived at dawn they found the stone rolled away, the tomb empty, and no Roman guard. The resurrection of our Lord, and His leaving the tomb had already taken place many hours earlier.

To complete our review of the events of every day, Nisan 9 through Nisan 18, Jesus appeared to Mary Magdalene, to two other disciples, and to the eleven at their Sunday evening dinner on that first resurrection day.

Meanwhile, back in Jerusalem certain members of the Roman guard were telling their story—the truth—to the Sanhedrin. They were bribed to lie that the disciples had stolen the body while they slept during the night hours of the first day of the week.

Three questions immediately come to mind about this story:

1. How could every member of a ten(?)-member Roman guard fall asleep at the same time?

2. How could every member of the guard remain asleep during the commotion of rolling away a stone to remove a corpse?

3. If every member of the guard was asleep, how did they know it was the disciples who stole the body?

These questions were apparently never asked of the guard, nor were they ever court marshaled for their dereliction of duty! But their bribe to lie was "commonly reported among the Jews until this day," (Matthew 28:11-15) and even until these last days before our Lord returns.

- -

Moreover brethren, I declare unto you the gospel which I preached unto you, which also ye have received, and wherein ye stand; by which also ye are saved, if you keep in memory what I preached unto you, unless ye have believed in vain. For I delivered unto you first of all that which I also received, how that Christ died for our sins according to the scriptures; and that he was buried, and that he rose again the third day according to the scriptures. I Corinthians 15:1-4.

CHAPTER 10

Nicodemus and Joseph Gave Us
The Greatest Proof

There are many "infallible proofs" for the resurrection from the dead of our Lord Jesus Christ. But the most convincing of all has gone overlooked and unproclaimed, except by the preacher and teacher who "is on the wrong side of just about everything, but right about it all." What is the most convincing proof? It is the conspiracy of Nicodemus and Joseph of Arimathea that is clearly chronicled in the inspired word of God.

I remember being taught when I was a boy, "If a doctrine or belief is mentioned only once in the Bible, that is sufficient for us to be assured that it is truth." (Significantly, Christ's...the Messiah's "thousand years" reign on earth is mentioned twice, and the "thousand years" period of time is mentioned six times!) Here are some of the proofs of Christ's resurrection cited often:

1. *The empty tomb.*
2. *Paul's inspired list of appearances.*
3. *The willingness of the disciples and other first century believers to face ridicule, persecution, and death for their proclamation of the resurrection.*
4. *The power of the risen Christ in the salvation of the lost and the building of His church during twenty centuries.*

But we never hear about the most convincing proof of all, the conspiracy of Nicodemus and Joseph of Arimathea. I never heard a sermon or had a Bible lesson about it. I searched the New Testament, and pondered this amazing story for many years. I found only a very few substantial hints of these pivotal events in the writings of only a very few scholars and authorities.

What follows is what the Holy Spirit taught me about one of the most astounding events recorded in the Word of God. And I must say, as kindly as I can under the circumstances, "Shame on a multitude of Bible teachers and preachers for overlooking and neglecting this mighty work of God accomplished by two Sanhedrin "insiders."

THE SANHEDRIN WITH MEMBERS JOSEPH AND NICODEMUS PROVIDE THE WORLD WITH THE GREATEST PROOF OF THE RESURRECTION OF OUR LORD JESUS CHRIST

Surely the wrath of man shall praise thee.
Psalm 76:10

The purpose of this message is to convince every reader that Almighty God used the growing faith and high position of Nicodemus, a "ruler of the Jews," and Joseph of Arimathea, "the rich man of Arimathea," to give to the world the greatest, most powerful and convincing evidence of the bodily resurrection of our Lord Jesus Christ to be found in the entire New Testament narrative.

This most convincing evidence didn't come from Jesus' disciples, or from His family, or from His Apostle Paul. It came from two *insiders* within the Jewish religious establishment—Nicodemus and Joseph—*who only* were in a position to demonstrate the fact either of Jesus' resurrection, or of His permanent death.

No one else could have done what Nicodemus and Joseph did to prove that Jesus rose from the dead. And God the Father, in His infinite wisdom and foreknowledge, knew it and planned it to be so. What those two Jewish Sanhedrin insiders did was neither coincidental nor accidental, or just a passing thought in the mind of God. I will be so bold as to say that it was planned from before the foundation of the world!

Nicodemus and Joseph knew exactly what they were doing, though they could not have known all the consequences of what they were doing.

Truly, "Surely the wrath of man shall praise thee." Psalm 76:10.

Are There Degrees of Wrath and Praise?

Since the truth of wrath and praise is declared so succinctly in the 76th Psalm, can we go further to infer that a smaller wrath will result in a smaller praise, while a larger wrath will result in a larger praise? I think we can.

Plotting against the life of the Son of God must have been the largest wrath of man, which, according to Psalm 76:10 will result in the greatest praise to God.

The greatest instance of man's wrath in the history of mankind will surely result in the greatest instance of praise to God in the history of mankind.

I may not have stated that great truth so eloquently or perfectly, but let's let it stand, and let us go on to this astonishing event in which Nicodemus and Joseph, were involved, and permit me to restate it this way:

The greatest example of man's wrath against God in all human history was the rejection and crucifixion of His Son.

Accordingly, the greatest example of that kind of wrath giving rise to the greatest praise to God in all human history is that that wrath led to the indisputable evidence of the resurrection of His Son.

"O the depth of the riches both of the wisdom and knowledge of God! How unsearchable are his judgments, and his ways past finding out!" Romans 11:33

Think of it!

Sinful men thought that they had done away with the Son of God once and for all. He was crucified. He died. He was buried. He would be dead and forgotten forever!

But at the very time that those evil hopes were filling the hearts and minds of those sinful men, two of their associates—insiders—were laying the basis for proof that would demonstrate forever that they did not succeed in their wrath against the Son of God, but that they themselves, by their actions, would enable their generation and all succeeding generations to know beyond any question or doubt that Jesus was not dead, and would not be forgotten forever, but instead, that He rose from the dead and was alive forevermore, to the eternal praise and glory of God the Father, God the Son, and God the Holy Spirit!

Please Pardon a Personal Note

In all my hearings of sermons and lectures on biblical topics, in all my readings, and in all my studies I have never seen this amazing story presented. Have I missed something?

Nicodemus and Joseph are invariably put in a bad light by preachers, teachers, and writers.

But it struck me one day while serving as a missionary in Japan, always seeking the words, the thoughts, and the truths to employ to convince the Japanese people to whom we ministered of the facts surrounding the death, burial and resurrection of our Lord Jesus Christ, and of the indisputable truth of this miracle—one of the two most amazing miracles of our Christian faith (the virgin birth and resurrection of our Lord)—that the story of Nicodemus and Joseph held the key.

The Holy Spirit impressed upon me the significance of the bribes that the chief priest and elders (the Sanhedrin) paid the soldiers to lie about the events of the resurrection. *Then suddenly I realized that the chief priests and elders had been set up; they had been trapped by the prior actions of two of their own—Nicodemus and Joseph!*

I then studied every word of scripture about Nicodemus and Joseph of Arimathea, and came to the conclusion that I have cherished ever since, *that God used His enemies (Nicodemus and Joseph not among them) to prove to the world the resurrection of His Son!*

How could the unfolding of this great truth found in the 76th Psalm in the events of the life, death, burial, and resurrection of our Lord Jesus Christ *not* have been understood and proclaimed for over 1900 years?

I don't know the answer to that question, but many years ago I knew that it was my duty to do the needed research and writing, to preach and teach it on the mission field in Japan, and from pulpits and through radio as God would give me opportunity.

In the early 1970s, I prepared a two-page exposition of this Old Testament truth with its New Testament fulfillment. I used it on the radio and distributed it to my listeners. But it vanished. I have searched everywhere for ten years, but it is gone.

Then this great truth struck me again. Aren't the frailties and wrath of man supposed to bring praise to God? Perhaps my first efforts, that I might have been satisfied with then, weren't pleasing to God. Does God want me to do it all over again, only to improve it the second time, I asked. (If there's anything I detest, it is doing something over that I have already done and misplaced!) Could this be another monumental effort of Satan, the enemy, to obscure and conceal this great truth?

Indeed! So here we are, on Palm Sunday, 1993, as we prepare to commemorate the events of the Passion Week in which Nicodemus and Joseph played such an important, but behind-the-scenes part. I have sat down to rewrite and improve, to do what I believe God wants me to do.

Who were Nicodemus and Joseph of Arimathea?

I used the word "enemies" a few paragraphs back. I was not referring to Nicodemus and Joseph. Though members of the Sanhedrin, they were friends and instruments of God. They were friends of the Son of God. By "enemies" I mean the wicked Jewish religious leaders whom they were associated with.

Have you ever thought of the fact that when our Lord talked with Nicodemus "by night," he knew that this man would be one of two who would bury him only three years later?

What can we glean from scripture about Nicodemus and Joseph?

Joseph of Arimathea

We will look at Joseph first because he played the more prominent role in the death, burial, and resurrection of our Lord, and because he may have been of higher rank than Nicodemus.

Joseph was the ultimate "insider." He was a "councilor of honorable estate." (Mark 15:42) He was a "rich man." (Matthew 27:57) And he was "a good man and a just." (Luke 23:50)

As a member of the Sanhedrin he knew about every discussion and deliberation concerning Jesus. He had the respect of his fellow Jerusalem establishment insiders.

Matthew, Mark, Luke, and John all give us insights concerning Joseph's spiritual condition. He was Jesus' disciple. (Matthew 27:57 and John 19:38) John adds that Joseph concealed his discipleship "for fear of the Jews." (John 19:38) But Luke informs us that Joseph "had not consented" to the decision of the Sanhedrin to condemn Jesus. (Luke 23:51)

While this incident reassures us that the Sanhedrin was not a monolithic totalitarian body, yet we have to be concerned for Joseph's welfare through it all. His interest in Jesus could not possibly have been totally secret.

Both Mark and Luke tell us that Joseph was "looking for the kingdom of God." (Mark 15:43 and Luke 23:51) This puts Joseph in the company of devout Jews like Simeon and Anna, who met the new born baby Jesus in the temple at Jerusalem, John the Baptist, Andrew and his brother Peter, and many others who were looking for the fulfillment of Old Testament prophecies.

If he had not been a high ranking member of the Jewish religious establishment, Joseph of Arimathea could not have had an audience with Pilate without notice or appointment. Moreover, if he had not been a high ranking religious leader he could not have had the authority to take the body of our Lord down from the cross and bury it on such short notice. "He boldly went in unto Pilate, and asked for the body of Jesus." (Mark 15:43) In this bold act, Joseph proved again that he was God's man—the right man in the right place at the right time—to bring praise to God out of the wrath of man.

Both Pilate and Joseph were witnesses to the report of the centurion that Jesus was indeed dead, not fainting, not in a swoon, not merely unconscious.

Pilate "granted the corpse to Joseph." (Mark 15:45)

Joseph then joined Nicodemus to wrap the body of our Lord in "a clean linen cloth" (Mark 15:46, Matthew 27:59, Luke 23:53, John 19:40) "with the spices." (John 19:40) All four Gospel writers tell us that Joseph, together with Nicodemus, then placed the body wrapped in linen with spices in Joseph's tomb. It was Joseph himself who "rolled a great stone to the door of the tomb." (Matthew 27:60, Mark 15:46, Luke 23:53, John 19:41) *Was this tomb one that Joseph had prepared for himself and his family, or was it prepared by Joseph for the burial of Jesus Christ in order to verify or disprove His resurrection predictions?*

Nicodemus

From the third chapter of John we know that Nicodemus was, like Paul, a Pharisee and a ruler of the Jews. Ruler means that he was a member of the Sanhedrin. He knew that Jesus was a "teacher come from God." He did not understand the truth of the new birth at his first meeting with Jesus, but he did indeed receive the Gospel message from the Way, the Truth, and the Life Himself, and I am convinced that somewhere along the way he believed and was saved.

In John 7:45-52 we find Nicodemus, again identified as a "Pharisee" and a "ruler," and "one of them" (no doubt referring to the Sanhedrin), dissenting from his fellow rulers in the condemnation of Jesus.

If Nicodemus was a member of the Sanhedrin, and I believe he was, then he is mentioned again by inference in Mark 15:1, Matthew 27:1, and Luke 22:66, when Jesus was brought before the chief priests, elders, and scribes at daybreak the morning after His arrest. Imagine the emotion that overwhelmed our Lord as He caught the eyes of Nicodemus and Joseph, knowing full well the role they were playing, and were to play in His burial and resurrection.

But let us keep in mind that if Nicodemus and Joseph were present on this terrible occasion, it was only to keep themselves informed and to be the two necessary witnesses to every event, not to participate in the condemnation of their Lord and Saviour.

The next and final biblical reference to Nicodemus is in the 19th chapter of John where we find him joining Joseph of Arimathea for the burial of Jesus. From this brief passage Nicodemus is described in these ways:

"He who at the first came to him by night."

That he brought to the tomb "a mixture of myrrh and aloes about a hundred pound weight."

That with Joseph "they took the body of Jesus, and bound it in linen cloths with the spices."

And that hurriedly they "laid Jesus" in the tomb because the Passover Sabbath was soon to begin (at sundown Wednesday).

This is what we know about Joseph and Nicodemus from the Gospel record.

Having buried Jesus, the next step to ensure the viability of their strategy was to tell their fellow rulers what they had done, and to request the Roman guard for the tomb! It was they who planted the idea in their minds to place the Roman seal and guard on the tomb. The authority to make such a request had to come from the entire Sanhedrin, though prompted by Joseph and Nicodemus.

This part of the account of Matthew is crucial to the strategy. Keep in mind that "the next day" meant after sundown Wednesday, before dark:

> "Now the next day, that followed the day of the preparation, the chief priests and Pharisees came together unto Pilate, saying, Sir, we remember that that deceiver said, while he was yet alive, after three days I will rise again. Command therefore that the sepulcher be made sure until the third day, lest his disciples come by night, and steal him away, and say unto the people, He is risen from the dead: so that the last error shall be worse than the first. Pilate said unto them, ye have a watch: go your way, and make it as sure as ye can. So they went, and made the sepulcher sure, sealing the stone, and setting a watch." (Matthew 27:62-66)

The trap was set! The Sanhedrin took the bait!

Joseph and Nicodemus probably did not know that God was using them to set this trap for the enemies of Jesus, but they set it nevertheless. They simply wanted to validate or invalidate Jesus' resurrection predictions.

It was a clever and commendable strategy. I do not disparage or condemn what Joseph and Nicodemus did, or their motives. God was simply using two Sanhedrin insiders to give us our most convincing proof of the resurrection of our Lord Jesus Christ.

And remember, what they did had to be disclosed, made public immediately. To have done anything in secret could have doomed their entire strategy.

Joseph's and Nicodemus' Attitude toward Jesus' Disciples

No doubt Joseph and Nicodemus had observed, and perhaps were even acquainted with Jesus' band of uneducated, devoted disciples. They also may have observed firsthand, or received reports of their behavior during the arrest and trial of Jesus, Judas' betrayal, Peter's denial, and the disciples' hiding out following the terrible events of the crucifixion. As a matter of fact, nothing could have been more convenient for Joseph and Nicodemus in the playing out of their strategy. They would not be bothered by the disciples.

It had become apparent during the fast paced events of the Day of Preparation before the Passover Sabbath (Tuesday sundown till Wednesday sundown) that Joseph and Nicodemus would not have to contend with any of Jesus' disciples or family over His body for the purposes of burial. They were nowhere to be found! Another evidence of God's hand in the events surrounding the death, burial, and resurrection of His Son!

In other words, Joseph and Nicodemus had a free hand to do whatever they wanted to do...*or better, what God wanted them to do*. This greatly facilitated the carrying out of their plan.

The Impact of Jesus' Words on His Disciples and on Joseph and Nicodemus

One of the most astonishing aspects of this saga is the fact that while Jesus' disciples apparently *forgot* His predictions of His resurrection from the dead, *Joseph and Nicodemus remembered.*

And Joseph and Nicodemus took advantage of this strange development, both in that Jesus' disciples were out of the picture, and not to be reckoned with, and in that they could use the fact that their fellow establishment friends knew that Jesus' disciples were out of the picture either to prove or disprove those predictions!

What a turn of events!

What an irony!

Jesus' disciples, who should have remembered, believed, and rejoiced in His promises of resurrection, were huddled together in fear!

Jesus' enemies (Joseph and Nicodemus not among them) did remember those predictions, however, and were out in the open boasting that such predictions would never come to pass, and that this Jesus could therefore be proved a liar and an imposter once and for all.

And in the middle, placed in their important positions by an omniscient God, were Joseph of Arimathea and Nicodemus, who also well remembered those predictions of resurrection, but who, because they had love and respect for, and faith in Jesus Christ, put their knowledge to an entirely different use.

And so we have three groups of people in this drama:

1. Jesus' disciples: Forgetting. Unbelieving. Fearing. Hiding.
2. Jesus enemies: Not forgetting. Rejoicing. Out in the open.
3. Joseph and Nicodemus: Not forgetting. Concerned. Wondering. Wanting to believe, but willing to disbelieve. Planning and plotting. And used—unbeknownst to them—by God to bring praise and glory out of wrath.

In order to totally understand Joseph's and Nicodemus' role in this drama, we must try to reconstruct the discussions, the decisions, and the events of the two or three hours during the burial of our Lord, through sundown (Wednesday) which marked the beginning of the Passover Sabbath, up until the time that darkness fell. Sundown would have been around 6:30, and the darkness an hour later.

After the Burial What to Do Next?

As they buried our Lord, Joseph and Nicodemus realized that they would have to meet with their fellow Sanhedrin members, and that they would have to have such a meeting quickly because sundown and the beginning of the Passover Sabbath was fast approaching.

In order to prevent everything they were doing from being done in secret, they had to report back to their colleagues of the Jerusalem establishment and to make their recommendation for the

Roman guard. (There is a question whether Joseph's burial of our Lord in his own tomb was or was not known and approved by the Sanhedrin prior to the event.)

Surely Joseph and Nicodemus were discussing, during their burial of our Lord, the necessity of the Roman guard as the only way to point conclusively to a resurrection event.

So while Jesus' many enemies were consumed by their wrath against God and His Son Jesus the Messiah, rejoicing in their great success in getting rid of Him and His disciples forever, Joseph of Arimathea and Nicodemus were approaching the "problem" in a more rational, logical, lawful, and godly manner.

Emergency Meeting of the Sanhedrin

At the very time that the Jews were making final preparations for their Passover Sabbath celebration—to begin at sundown, "the next day," Nisan 15, our Wednesday evening till Thursday evening—the Sanhedrin had some important business before them. I repeat, this meeting took place shortly after sundown, "the next day." The main business was to hear from Joseph and Nicodemus about the burial of our Lord, and to discuss the possible theft of His body by His disciples.

Whenever this crucial meeting took place, the Sanhedrin was clearly alarmed at the prospect of a theft of Jesus' body by His disciples. But they were no doubt pleased that two of their own had taken care of the burial. Likewise, they may have been puzzled why Joseph would waste a new tomb on the likes of Jesus of Nazareth.

Nevertheless, they all—including Joseph and Nicodemus no doubt guiding the discussion—realized that the only way that it could be proved conclusively and forever that the body of Jesus would remain in the tomb and not be stolen by the disciples was to have a Roman guard of several soldiers stationed at the entrance of the tomb for three days and three nights, beginning Wednesday night.

Summary of Joseph's and Nicodemus' Report to the Sanhedrin

Joseph and Nicodemus undoubtedly reported the following to as many members of the Sanhedrin as could be gathered together at that very inopportune time: (1) To affirm that they had ascertained beyond any question that Jesus had died on the cross, (2) to confirm that they had received approval from Pilate to bury the body, (3) to confirm that they had indeed buried the body of our Lord in a tomb owned by Joseph himself, (4) to suggest that since Jesus had predicted His resurrection, surely His disciples were at that very moment plotting to steal the body, dispose of it, and then claim that He had risen from the dead, and (5) to insist that in order to prevent such a calamity taking place they, the Sanhedrin, should appeal to Pilate to place a Roman guard of several soldiers at the entrance of the tomb. (Joseph and Nicodemus, possibly knowing of the disciples' hiding away, might have concluded that they were at that very moment plotting the theft of the body from Joseph's tomb. But they could not know for sure.)

The Sanhedrin Convinced, They Go to Pilate

The following scriptures are so important that I am repeating them. Remember that "the next day" means after sundown, the beginning of the next day on the Hebrew calendar, which in this instance was Wednesday evening after sundown, but no doubt before dark.

"Now the next day, that followed the day of the preparation, the chief priests and Pharisees came together unto Pilate, saying, Sir, we remember that that deceiver said, while he was yet alive, after three days I will rise again. Command therefore that the sepulcher be made sure until the third day, lest his disciples come by night, and steal him away, and say unto the people, He is risen from the dead: so that the last error shall be worse than the first. Pilate said unto them, ye have a watch: go your way, and make it as sure as ye can. So they went, and made the sepulcher sure, sealing the stone, and setting a watch." (Matthew 27:62-66)

The trap was sprung. The Sanhedrin trapped themselves!

The Resurrection of Our Lord Sometime
Between Sundown Saturday and Sunrise Sunday

The language of both the Greek and English are somewhat obscure, but we can piece together these events:

1. The women who were most interested in paying their respects at the tomb visited the tomb after sundown Saturday, marking the end of the seventh day Sabbath. (Mark 16:1 and Matthew 28:1) This was the beginning of the first day of the week.

2. After they left, at sometime during the darkness, perhaps before midnight, there was an earthquake, and an angel appeared like lightning and rolled away the stone from the tomb. The members of the Roman guard witnessed this spectacular event, they trembled, and fell to the ground "as dead men." (Matthew 28:2-4)

3. Just before dawn on Sunday morning the women, not knowing about the spectacular events of the night, returned to the tomb. By this time the members of the Roman guard had recovered from their unconscious state, and were on their way to tell the Sanhedrin (not their Roman superiors!) what happened. (Mark 16:2, Luke 24:1, John 20:1)

4. The women found the stone rolled away from the tomb and a young man inside "sitting on the right side, clothed in a long white garment." (Mark 16:5) Two men were also standing by them "in shining garments." (Luke 24:4) The young man who was sitting explained what had happened, and gave the women instructions.

We will skip over the other reports and conversations among the disciples, as well as the various appearances of Jesus to his family, friends, and disciples, to the culmination of Joseph's and Nicodemus' strategy.

The Guard Honestly Reported What They Knew
Had Taken Place

"Some of the watch came into the city, and showed unto the chief priests all the things that were done." (Matthew 24:11)

These Roman soldiers had no reason to lie. The record does not tell us that the chief priests disbelieved them.

The soldiers should have been fearful about several things: (1) Not carrying out their mission. (2) Lying about it and being discovered to have lied. And (3) punishment for dereliction of duty and/or lying. They surely did not take this matter lightly.

Though the Soldiers Did Not Lie,
The Sanhedrin Bribed Them to Lie!

In order to conceal and dispel any notion of a miraculous, spectacular event in which Jesus might have risen from the dead, the chief priests, scribes, Pharisees, and elders—*the Sanhedrin*—gave the soldiers large amounts of money to tell a different story about the events of the night. They simply could not risk having the soldiers tell others of the spectacular happenings that put them on the ground unconscious.

These are the ingredients of the lie they were bribed to tell:

1. That they all were asleep at the same time at some point during the night.
2. That while they were all asleep the disciples came to steal the body.
3. That the disciples stole the body.

Such a story, of course, was an admission of guilt on the part of the soldiers—all sleeping at the same time while on duty, allowing the very thing to happen that they were supposed to prevent!

So to protect the guard from sure punishment by the Roman authorities, the influential Sanhedrin promised that they would "persuade him and secure you" (with more money perhaps?). Matthew adds this telling sentence, "This saying is commonly reported among the Jews until this day." (Matthew 28:15)

Joseph's and Nicodemus' plan had worked beyond their wildest expectation! Not only would the soldiers tell the truth someday, the Sanhedrin had implicated and complicated themselves beyond all repair.

Only Limited Success for the Sanhedrin

We can surmise that the Sanhedrin was successful in the cover-up *only up to a point*. That the guard was never court marshaled for their dereliction of duty surely must have raised some first century eyebrows.

But more embarrassing to the Sanhedrin, when it was discovered that they had bribed the guard to lie, were three questions that every thinking person was asking:

1. How could a group of well-trained Roman soldiers have all fallen asleep at the same time while on guard duty?
2. How could not even one of them been awakened by the commotion of a robbery in progress, involving a group of men moving a large stone, then carrying a body away.
3. *If every member of the guard was asleep at the same time, how were they able to identify the thieves as Jesus' disciples?*

Great Success for Joseph and Nicodemus

At this point in our description of this drama we can afford to repeat for the emphasis it deserves: Joseph's and Nicodemus' strategy was successful beyond their fondest hope. The deals between the Sanhedrin and the soldiers were a bonus, and seemed to reinforce the evidence for the resurrection of our Lord Jesus Christ that Joseph and Nicodemus so cleverly and masterfully established.

All Witnesses Were Interviewed

I believe that Joseph and Nicodemus, as well as the soldiers who guarded the tomb became prime witnesses interviewed by the Gospel writers, Matthew, Mark, Luke, and John. Surely other disciples and writers of scripture like Peter, James, Jude, and Paul sought out Joseph and Nicodemus, and thus learned of these great events from firsthand insider witnesses. Who could corroborate the story of the assignment of the guard to watch the tomb, followed by the story of the bribing of the soldiers to lie better than two men who observed those events firsthand?

Apparently, the soldiers did not keep their promise to lie forever, because events that only they knew had happened were recorded by Matthew for all to read for nearly 2,000 years.

What exciting interviews those must have been between the soldiers and the New Testament writers! With every interview they must have shaken their heads in astonishment at what Joseph, Nicodemus, the Sanhedrin, and the soldiers had accomplished, and thanked God for them all. That's why Peter could say with boldness on Pentecost just 47 days later, "Him, being delivered by the determinate counsel and foreknowledge of God, ye have taken, and by wicked hands have crucified and slain: Whom God hath raised up, having loosed the pains of death: because it was not possible that he should be holden of it." (Acts 2:23-24)

Surely the Wrath of Man Shall Praise Thee. Psalm 76:10

This brings us back to our starting point: The wrath of the enemies of our Lord Jesus Christ (1) to crucify Him, (2) to support their insider friends, Joseph and Nicodemus who buried Him, (3) to secure a Roman guard from the Roman authorities to prevent Jesus' disciples from stealing His body, and finally (4) to bribe the soldiers to lie, all brought praise and glory to God in a most dramatic way. In every respect they were displaying their wrath; likewise in every respect they brought praise and glory to God.

Yes, indeed, the enemies of Jesus Christ, entrapped by two of His friends among them, provided us with our greatest proof for the empty tomb! No one else could have done it as they did.

Lessons

There are so many lessons for us in this strange but thrilling story.

Sometimes it seems as though everything is going wrong, but God sees beyond the calamity. For example:

One of the darkest days in our entire lives was the day (January 1, 1988) the Maryland rabbi attempted to take custody of the remains of our dear Jewish Christian friend Haviv Schieber, after I had promised him that he would have a Christian funeral and be buried with this Christian friends. We had to spend two weeks in court and $2,000. But the judge ruled in our favor. The story was on the front page of every newspaper in the Washington area, and went out on the news wire services around the world. Jesus Christ was honored and glorified in a way that would have been impossible had we had a quiet, uneventful funeral.

Another lesson is that we must not be overly judgmental, certainly not condemnatory, of fellow believers who don't seem to be serving our Lord in exactly the same way as we do. Joseph and Nicodemus are often accused of not following Jesus openly "for fear of the Jews," or for coming to Jesus in the darkness of night. But God's hand was upon them, and they were being prepared to provide the world with the only totally legal evidence for the resurrection of our Lord Jesus Christ.

Of course, there will never again be such an important task for which God will need "secret" or "fearful" followers of Jesus. So we are not making excuses for such conduct. But we do not diminish the sovereignty of God by saying that He needed, and had prepared two men like Joseph and Nicodemus to perform such a great task. He can use the most unlikely to accomplish His purposes.

"O the depth of the riches both of the wisdom and knowledge of God! How unsearchable are his judgments, and his ways past finding out." (Romans 11:33) "Surely the wrath of man shall praise thee." (Psalm 76:10) "And we know that all things work together for good to them that love God, to them who are the called according to his purpose." (Romans 8:28)

CHAPTER 11

Evolutionism and Creation, Not Evolution and Creationism

◆══◯══◆

*N*itpicking? No, not all. One of the reasons we have lost so many battles in the war against error is that we have fought the enemy on his terms. A good example of this in the struggle against evolutionism is the evolutionists' use of the word "theory." Evolutionism has not yet reached the status of a good theory, so why should we let them get away with talking about their theory of evolution? We lose ground unnecessarily when we make such concessions and accommodations.

I have debated and argued against the wild unscientific conjectures of evolutionism from young manhood—in high school, in Japan, in Hawaii, on the "Right Start for the Day" radio program since the 1940s, and on "The King's Business" radio program since 1979.

Again I have found myself "on the wrong side" of a few issues and disputes with my fellow ministers and colleagues, but as usual, "right about it all." I will touch on these three important matters in this message:

1. Neither evolutionism nor creation are subjects for scientific treatment.
2. Since neither is a subject for scientific treatment, neither has a place in a science classroom or in a museum of science.
3. Believers in the biblical truth of creation should stop using unbelievers' terminology: "evolution and creationism." The proper terminology for believers is "evolutionism and creation."

We can address and dispense with the first point at the outset, simply and briefly. In order to qualify as a topic or *object of scientific treatment, the topic or object must be subject to three basic steps of scientific investigation (also known as "the scientific method").*

Step one. There must be firsthand observation by human investigators. Step two. There must be generalizations (hypothetical rules governing the natural phenomenon or phenomena being observed). And step three. There must be predictions and experimentation in order to test the generalizations arrived at in step two.

Both evolutionism and creation fail at every step. Neither is a proper subject of scientific study. Both must be accepted by faith.

No one was present to observe the alleged process of evolution over millions of years, nor was anyone present when God created the heavens and the earth. Since firsthand observation is impossible for both evolutionism and creation, it is therefore impossible to proceed to steps two and three.

This simple bit of straight thinking led me to oppose the popular movement among Christians some thirty years ago known as "The Two-Model Approach," so I broadcast and published a message entitled, "Seven Evils of the Two-Model Approach." That movement is pretty much a thing of the past, but since it continues to surface in various forms from time to time (i.e. "Intelligent Design" alongside evolution in science classes), I am including it in this study.

And since evolutionism is not science I testified before a Congressional committee on February 18th, 1981, that the taxpayers of the United States should not be required to pay for the teaching of the religion of evolutionism in both the Air and Space Museum and the National Museum of Natural History. (Though we didn't achieve total victory in this protest, some of the more outrageous displays promoting evolutionism can no longer be found in the museums.) The text of that testimony is also included in this message.

On point number three I beg my fellow Bible believers and Christians to stop using unbelievers' terminology, "evolution and creationism," and instead use only the truth-

ful terminology as a weapon in this struggle, which is "evolutionism and creation."

Though not always, the English suffix "-ism" sometimes denotes and implies questionable dogma. The questionable dogma is evolutionism. Creation is the truth. When the two words are used in the same sentence, or in the same thought, the "-ism" should always be attached to "evolution" and never to "creation."

"On the wrong side of just about everything, but right about it all."

- -

Through the years some of my listeners and readers have wondered how I got involved so deeply and so passionately in the evolutionism/creation controversy. I can explain that in a very few paragraphs.

First, I was born with an inquiring mind and spirit. Although I believed what my parents and teachers taught me, I questioned everything. I wanted to be a scientist. I could have been a good scientist.

Second, my father led a protest against professors who were teaching evolutionism at Baylor University in 1923, two years before the famous Scopes trial in Tennessee. It turned in to a complex and difficult affair, in which even Governor Neff was involved, because he was a Baylor trustee. After two years my father was victorious, and seven professors who taught the lies of evolutionism at that Baptist university were dismissed.

It was an exciting story that my brother and I liked to hear our father tell in the 1930s and 1940s. He had slain the foul dragon of evolutionism at Baylor University, and he was our hero. I am certain that one of the reasons I have carried on where he left off is out of love, admiration, and loyalty to him.

And third, above all of course, the Bible teaches creation, and mentions the God of creation and salvation many, many times from Genesis to Revelation. There is not one scientific proof for evolutionism (see the paragraphs on scientific methodology above). The Bible does not lie, but evolutionism is a monumental system of deception built around rebellion against our Creator and Saviour, preconceived and unproveable notions, and lies and hoaxes of all kinds.

- -

Now, by way of introduction to my "Seven Evils of the Two-Model Approach," and "Seven Reasons Why Taxpayers Should Not Pay for Unscientific Displays in Museums of Science," I want to relate one of the defining experiences of my life: How one of my favorite school teachers taught me evolutionism, but apologized to me 37 years later, after she had become a strong Bible-believing Christian and Christian school principal.

An Unhappy Encounter with Evolutionism in 1939 With a Happy, Emotional Ending 37 Years Later in 1976

I had just ended three blissful years in the 3rd, 4th, and 5th grades at Peabody School on Capitol Hill when I was told that I would be transferred to the Hilton School, just a block away, for the 6th grade.

I was devastated. Summer vacation 1939 was miserable as I contemplated leaving Peabody to go to Hilton. This change was probably explained to my parents (but not to me), that I had been selected to be one of twenty students in a special class to be taught by one of Washington's up-and-coming rising stars for my 6th grade teacher, Miss Elizabeth Newsome.

Most of the boys and girls in this new class were also from Peabody, so that made it easier—David Gould, Frank Noell, Frances Kaufman, Norma Evenson, Dorothy Major, Joan Frederick, and the Cartwright girls from Oklahoma. It wasn't long before I was happy again, especially as I got to know my beautiful and wonderful new teacher. I loved and respected her, and did my best to please her with good grades and good behavior.

But while my lessons had been a breeze for me from the 3rd through the 5th grades at Peabody, I really had to work hard to keep up with all the smart girls in that new class, because Miss Newsome graded on the curve.

Moreover, being a Christian boy from a strict Christian home, and a member of a strong Bible believing church only a block away—Metropolitan Baptist Church—I was downhearted every time Miss Newsome would teach us evolutionism in the science hour. I knew she was wrong, and it hurt, because I could never answer the test questions on evolutionism the way I was supposed to. I remember once trying to explain to her why I couldn't give the "right answer" on some test questions.

Then one day in the spring of 1940 Miss Newsome gave us the exciting news that we were going on a science trip to the National Museum of Natural History. I had already been there with our family, but I never saw enough of our marvelous Smithsonian Institution museums. I remember on the day of our visit to the museum that Miss Newsome seemed especially eager during our walk through the hall of evolution to help us understand what we were seeing.

There were displays of dinosaurs evolving into pretty little birds, a frog-like sea creature crawling up out of the water on to land, with his evolving new legs and…then …THERE HE WAS, THE PILT-DOWN MAN! Yes, dear listener and reader, believe it or not, this monumental hoax of the evolutionists was on prominent display in the National Museum of Natural History in the 1930s and 1940s. I remember that Miss Newsome called her class's attention to this concocted ape man. (The Piltdown Man was proved to be a hoax in the 1950s and removed from the museum. I have a photograph of it in an earlier proud publication of the Smithsonian Institution.)

Inside my little 12-year old mind I snickered. I had been taught the truth of the Word of God about the creation of earth's plant and animal life, and I knew the Piltdown Man was a fake. By that time I was already asking such questions, "Where are the Piltdown Men today who are just now finally evolving into human beings?" and "Why aren't there strange looking just-evolving creatures all over the world?"

Well, I finished the 6th grade with a good report card, and said "Goodbye" to my dear Miss Newsome.

One Sunday 37 years later, in the Bicentennial Year of our nation's Declaration of Independence, I was the guest preacher at the Bible Baptist Church of Clinton, Maryland, where my friend from childhood, John Macon, was pastor. That was the church where the famous Clinton Christian School was located, established and built so successfully by Pastor Macon.

Having just returned from Japan and Hawaii, I delivered a straightforward message on world evangelization.

At the close of the service I stood with the pastor at the entrance of the church building to greet the congregation as they left.

An attractive older woman, in her late sixties, took my hand, squeezed it firmly, looked me straight in the eye, and said with emotion and tears in her eyes, "Dale, I was your sixth grade teacher, and I want to apologize to you for teaching you evolution. I thought it was my duty to convince everyone in your class of evolution. But I am a Christian now, and I know evolution is wrong."

By the time she finished speaking to me, tears were falling down my face. I said, "Miss Newsome," and hugged her. I couldn't say anything else.

I have wished many times through the years that had followed up on that wonderful reunion with another visit to Miss Newsome's new principal's office, but I was "too busy," as usual.

I learned from Pastor Macon that Miss Newsome was led to Christ by Frank Noell's mother, that she had married a doctor, who was unfaithful to her, and that she was now the principal of the Clinton Christian School. He also told me that she had an amazing knowledge of the Bible, knowing many passages from memory, and that during her years as a Washington, D.C. public school teacher she achieved the distinction of "eminently superior teacher" many times. I wonder how much of the success of my ministry, and how much the content even of this book can be attributed to that unforgettable year in Miss Newsome's sixth grade class.

- -

Miss Elizabeth Newsome's Special Sixth Grade Class
At Hilton Elementary School on Capitol Hill in Washington, D.C., 1939
Miss Newsome was determined to convince every student about evolutionism,
but she apologized to Dale Jr. 37 years later, after she had become a Christian.
Dale is second from right.

Indeed, "On the wrong side of just about everything, but right about it all" has been one of the trademarks of my life, even at the age of twelve. This compilation of radio and print messages would not be complete without these two memorable experiences from 1939 and 1976. Again, I was on the wrong side of my favorite teacher, but proved to be right 37 years later.

Now read on about two more encounters with error in the conflict between evolutionism and creation.

Seven Evils of the Two-Model Approach

Here are the seven reasons why you will never hear me promoting the two-model approach to the teaching of evolutionism and creation in the science classes of our public, monopolistic, tax-supported schools.

1. Biblical Separation

"Have no fellowship with the unfruitful works of darkness, but rather reprove them." (Ephesians 5:11) Evolutionism is an unfruitful work of darkness. To spend God's money (which you have been encouraged to do), and to devote any of our time and talents to the preparation of materials and training of teachers to teach evolutionism is clearly having "fellowship with the unfruitful works of darkness."

When some Christian leaders not only accept, but promote this so-called "two model approach," endorsing the poison alongside the truth, not so bad?" How about a two model approach for Communism and Americanism? For free sex and Biblical sex? Would it not be just as reasonable?

We should be reproving evolutionism—not trying to find ways to make it palatable, alongside the truth of creation, to the ungodly educators and bureaucrats of our society. How can a Christian teacher in a government school teach the "evolution model," and thus have fellowship with an unfruitful work of darkness in an environment sympathetic to that unfruitful work of darkness?

2. Christian Naiveté

We display our naiveté and foolishness to think that we are going to achieve a fair presentation of both the creation an evolution "models" in our public schools. Jesus said, "the children of this world are in their generation wiser than the children of light." (Luke 16:8) The children of this world are militantly anti-Creator. Why should the children of light go hat-in-hand to them, begging their approval of our "two model approach?"

Do we really think that a Christian teacher in a secular school will give a fair, unbiased presentation of the "evolution model?" And do we really think that a non-Christian teacher will give a fair, unbiased presentation of the "creation model?"

3. Spiritual Discernment

We display the paucity of our spiritual discernment to think that the great majority of unspiritual school teachers will convince even a few students of the spiritual truth of creation. The natural man receiveth not the things of the Spirit of God for they are foolishness unto him neither can he know them, because they are spiritually discerned." (I Cor. 2:14) Creation is one of those spiritually discerned truths of God. Do we really believe that the "creation model" as presented by the non-Christian teacher, who does not possess the Holy Spirit can be perceived by even a few of our precious boys and girls in a hostile environment?

If we believe that we flunk the spiritual discernment test.

4. Devious Tactics

There is a time and a place for the children of light to be wise as serpents, but who do we think we are fooling when we present our two-model approach to the humanistic, evolutionistic education community? The world is totally aware of our transparent efforts to disguise our creation curriculum in the "two-model approach," reassuring them of our willingness to teach evolution too. We bring no credit to ourselves, nor honor to our Lord through such tactics.

When we should be on the front lines of battle, fighting the good fight of faith, we are instead sneaking around in the shadows, playing word games with the enemy.

5. A Humanist Approach

I wish the best for our government schools, and I hope that they can be improved, and regain the ground lost in recent years. But is it the responsibility of Godly parents and leaders to patch up a man-made, God forsaken secularistic, humanistic school system? Jesus said, "No man putteth a piece of new cloth unto an old garment... neither do men put new wine into old bottles." (Matthew 9:16,17) How can the sound cloth of creation truth be patched into a system shot through with evolutionistic and humanistic error? By so doing will we not find ourselves aiding and abetting the very humanism that we decry?

We ought to be using our time and talents, and the contributions of God's people to establish Christian schools—the new wine-skins—where Christian teachers can teach creation freely in the power of the Holy Spirit, and where multitudes of precious boys and girls can receive their Creator's love and grace, and forgiveness of sin, and be saved.

God does not need our attempts to save the world's crumbling institutions in order to give His "little ones" a fair opportunity to choose between creation and evolutionism. We ought to be spreading the truth, not lies, trusting the Lord of the harvest to give the increase. "It is never right to do wrong in order to get a chance to do right."

6. Aberrations and Excesses

I will not elaborate on this problem of the advocates of the "two-model approach."

A double minded ("two model"?) man is unstable in all his ways." (James 1:8)

7. Path of Compromise

Is the "two-model approach" but another attempt on the part of Bible believers to make our religious beliefs palatable to the world?

I am afraid that we want to prove to the debaters, the skeptics, the atheists, and the bureaucrats of this world that we are reasonable people with something to offer and in the process we have been led down the path of compromise, weakening the very testimony we set out to establish in the first place.

EXCERPT OF TESTIMONY
Before the House of Representatives Subcommittee
On the Department of Interior and Related Agencies
SEVEN REASONS
Why Evolutionism Should Not Be Advanced with Public Funds
In Two Museums of the Smithsonian Institution
Witness: Dale Crowley Jr., President
National Heritage Foundation
February 18, 1981

First Reason. By definition, a museum is a place where facts, artifacts, inventions, discoveries, fossils, and other tangible items are assembled and displayed. Speculations about evolution are merely abstract conjectures about the origin of the universe and life on earth. These conjectures, when asserted to be factual, are out of place in a museum.

Second Reason. The curators of the National Museum of Natural History should confine their displays to natural history. The conjectured processes of evolution are unknown in nature today. Furthermore, evolution deals with prehistory—speculation about what took place before man could observe natural phenomena and record those observations.

Third Reason. The curators of the Air and Space Museum should confine their displays to air and space as we know it today and since the beginning of scientific investigation. The origin of the universe has no relevance or application to the exploration of earth's atmosphere and space beyond.

Fourth Reason. The two museums that are the subject of my testimony are museums of science (as opposed to a museum of art). The definition of science that we are dealing with here includes the processes of observation, generalization, and verification, all performed by human beings. Therefore, by definition, the alleged processes of evolution, that allegedly took place millions and billions of years ago, cannot be included within the rubric of science. That is, (1) observation of the prehistoric processes of evolution by human beings was impossible, (2) generalizations cannot be made, and (3) verification is thus impossible. It is a travesty of science to feature such unobservable, un-generalize-able, and unverifiable conjecture in a museum of science. Clearly, evolution is a matter of faith, not science.

Fifth Reason. Museums, especially the two that are the subject of this testimony, are powerful tools of instruction and indoctrination. People enter a museum with a mindset to accept what they see, read, and hear, without question. It is inappropriate, unbecoming, and unworthy of a museum of science, therefore, to take unfair advantage of the public by purporting to present only facts, artifacts, and the results of scientific investigation, when in reality the evolutionary displays in those museums have not and cannot be supported through scientific investigation. It is nothing short of scandalous that the prestigious museums of the Smithsonian Institution would be guilty of deliberately misleading the public, presenting mere philosophical speculation as scientific discovery.

Sixth Reason. There is a great and growing controversy among scientists about the assumptions and conclusions of evolutionary speculation. (Such controversy, of course, is totally absent from the most basic discoveries of scientific investigation.) Hundreds of Doctors of Science and Philosophy, professors, and researchers in every field of science not only question the assumptions and conclusions of evolution, but they dismiss them out-of-hand as far removed from the boundaries of true science. Therefore it is most unworthy of a handful of Smithsonian Institution scientists to continue to preempt every dissenting viewpoint, and to insist upon presenting evolutionary conjecture as scientific discovery to 20 million visitors annually.

Seventh Reason. Finally, there are millions of Americans whose faith is in an alternative view of origins; namely, specific, direct creation. How unfair it is to take the tax dollars of these loyal Americans to indoctrinate their fellow Americans in an unverifiable conjecture as fact—a conjecture that they themselves not only do not believe, but which they actively oppose and protest.

The wrongness of all of this illogic, inconsistency, and injustice is compounded by the fact that Congress has, through the years, appropriated hundreds of millions of dollars to support it all.

I beg you to take appropriate action to terminate this unwise, wasteful, unjust use of public funds.

CHAPTER 12

The Gospel to Iraq, Not Bombs, Guns, and Bullets—Support the Troops, Impeach Their Leaders

⊷⇒◉⇐⊷

Back in the 1940s a good Christian wouldn't dare say such a thing, either on the radio or in print. One of the popular unsound doctrines of the early decades of the 1900s, and one that I found myself on the wrong side of slightly in the '40s and '50s, and mightily later, was that true, ideal Christians should be so dedicated ("dedicated" was a big word for Christians in those days) to the work of Christ and His church that they had no time for Caesar, human government, or politics.

This pernicious approach to Christian citizenship took various forms.

We were taught by some highly respected leaders that since the Gospel was the answer to all of man's problems, we should use our time and talents 100 percent witnessing for Christ. That if we were totally dedicated to God we should have nothing left over for Caesar. That spending any portion of our lives on the temporary affairs of nations was a foolish waste, the opposite of laying up treasures in heaven.

Therefore rendering unto Caesar what belonged to Caesar came down to...well...nothing...except, of course, taxes.

Now before going any further with this, I want to pause to remind my listeners that I didn't learn any of the foregoing unsound doctrine from my father. He was very much involved in "ministry to Caesar," to put it mildly. He used his gifts of preaching and teaching, via radio and the printed page, to upbraid Caesar when he thought Caesar needed upbraiding, to lecture politicians on their errors and evils, as well as good government, to expose ungodliness in high places, and to make every effort possible within his God-given resources, to cause Caesar to conform to the will of God.

He addressed government leaders by name in his radio broadcasts. He wrote and published letters to presidents. He sent open letters to every member of Congress on various issues vital to the spiritual, moral, financial, and military well-being of America. He was one of the early twentieth century crusaders for good government and against bad government.

President Truman told "Washington's Radio Minister" that he listened to the "Right Start for the Day" program every morning possible. Dale Crowley had the ear and the respect of Supreme Court justices, and other molders of opinion in Washington and nationwide. Yes, I learned militant Christianity in the arena of Christ's church and human government from my father.

- - - - - - - - - - - - -

Returning now to the thoughts which began this message—the unsound doctrines we were taught in the early decades of the twentieth century—to sum it up: The idea was that our American government (and overall way of life) was so good, so right, so pleasing to God, so in harmony with His will, that we Christians, to be really good Christians, must be compliant, subservient and obedient in every respect. This was "rendering to Caesar what belonged to Caesar and to God what belonged to God."

I remember sitting in a Bible study class one Sunday morning when this very doctrine of the Christian's proper role in the world was being discussed. One of the students asked the teacher, "What if the government ordered me to kill my mother? What should I do?"

The answer came, without blinking or hesitation: "You should obey the government, because government is ordained of God, and we as Christians must not be disobedient. God will then avenge your mother's murder as He deals with the government."

I was a little skeptical of that answer, as I was already moving in the direction of being "on the wrong side of just about everything."

One of the most frequently heard mantras of the '30s and '40s relative to all of this was, "Don't criticize anyone in government. No matter the wrongdoing or the wrongdoer, we must show our respect."

- - - - - - - - - - - - -

It's time now to examine the outcome of all this unsound doctrine regarding what belongs to God and what belongs to Caesar. Several volumes could be written, but I'll sum it up in a few paragraphs.

Well, you can imagine, this is the politicians and the officials dream come true. They were laughing all the way to their offices every morning. Nothing could be better than for the preachers and for the Christians to keep quiet, show their respect, obey orders, and pay their taxes.

They did exactly what "principalities and powers in high places" are destined to do best—turn a once Christian nation over to the devil. We could almost hear them congratulating one another, "No matter what we do those Christians and churches will support us. They won't be complaining one whit."

And Satan? Well, he had a field day for several decades of the 1900s, as he subverted and took over a once Christian nation, turning it in to one of the most lawless nations in human history. By their silence and tacit approval, Christians actually contributed to the consignment of a nation to hell.

By the time of the Supreme Court's prayer and Bible reading decision of 1963, and the legalization of baby murder of 1973, it was too late. The HIV virus of Christian complacency and compliance had morphed into full blown immune deficiency against sin, evil, crime, and corruption. For thirty years the momentum of lawlessness has been of greater force than the majority's morality.

- - - - - - - - - - - - -

In conclusion to this introduction to my message in opposition to the invasion and occupation of Iraq, I want to ask a few questions. The first question is prompted by my meeting Japanese pastors who were punished by their government for not obeying certain edicts during World War II. The government had ordered every church in the land to place a photograph of the emperor on or near the pulpit, before which the congregation must bow in respect and worship at the beginning of every service. Most churches complied, but a few did not. Those who disobeyed this order were punished severely. They were the heroes in post-war Japan. They refused to bow down.

- - - - - - - - - - - - -

Now its question time.

This first-term missionary to Japan had to ask himself the obvious questions: Does God have two standards of obedience to His law—a lower standard for American Christians who are special, and one for Japanese Christians who are not so special? Why is it wonderful for Japanese Christians who have the courage to disobey Caesar, but awful for American Christians to do the same? Were those Christians, pastors, and churches that defied Hitler's lawlessness out of the will of God?

Back to the U.S.A., and those advocates of subservience.

Had they forgotten that thirteen colonies rebelled against their legally established authorities in England? Didn't they know that the driving force behind the war for independence was defiance of the crown? Had they never read the history of Christian support for what we now know as the Revolutionary War? (I have a marvelous book given to me by one of my King's Business partners, a book of sermons preached by militant pastors, urging rebellion against British tyranny.)

Had they never read the Declaration of Independence by which this once Christian nation got its start by the grace, and the in favor of God? Don't they know that the very government and nation that they say we should be totally subservient to had its origin in this kind of defiance, reproach, disrespect, and rebellion? The Declaration, written and edited partly by the Christian, John Adams, is full of contempt and insubordination:

"...abuses and usurpations..."

"...absolute Despotism..."

"The history of the present King of Great Britain is a history of repeated injuries and usurpations, all having in direct object the establishment of an absolute Tyranny over these States."

"...he has utterly neglected..."

"...the sole purpose of fatiguing them into compliance..."

"...his invasion on the rights of the people..."

"...He has erected a multitude of New Offices, and sent hither swarms of Officers to harass our people, and eat out their substance." (Sound familiar? My favorite sentence in the list of grievances.)

"He has plundered our seas, ravaged our Coasts, burnt our towns, and destroyed the lives of our people."

"...the works of death, desolation and tyranny..."

"...a tyrant...unfit to be a ruler..."

In all honesty we must remember that there were Bible believing Christian patriots in the 1700s who believed, as many do today, that it is wrong to disrespect and disobey government authority. At the same time we must remember that had their beliefs prevailed there would never have come into being a United States of America.

To help resolve the dilemma of the Declaration of Independence from a Christian perspective, we need only go to the writings of John Locke (1632-1704) and Edmund Burke (1729-1797), two fervent Christian philosophers and jurists of England, who taught that it was citizens' right to throw off tyranny, and their duty to do so, if they could, of course. Our Founding Fathers quoted from the writings of

Locke and Burke more frequently than from any other source, except the Bible.

Now we go to the word of God for a final look at the probity, the rightness of defiance and disobedience of citizens against government authority. An honest look at these biblical instances should settle the matter once and for all.

Since this is question time, again I ask the question: Didn't those sanctimonious Christian patriots of the first half of the 1900s know that the following incidents actually happened in Bible times?

Moses defied and disobeyed Pharaoh. The outcome was liberty, five books of the Bible, and all that followed.

Nathan rebuked King David.

Elijah was constantly at odds with Ahab and Jezebel. He had no use for them. At a final showdown he mocked and did away with Ahab's pagan priests.

After King Jehoshaphat had collaborated with Ahab in a battle against Assyria, an obscure prophet met him on the way back to Jerusalem and admonished him, "Shouldest thou help the ungodly, and love them that hate the Lord? Therefore is wrath upon thee from before the Lord." (Sound familiar? Good men in the White House shouldn't go out and fight wars on behalf of ungodly nations. And men and women of God need to tell them so.)

Jeremiah predicted the defeat of the Jews by the Babylonians, urged the king not to go to war, was accused of demoralizing the troops, and treason, and thrown in a dirty pit. Is there any indication in the Bible that Jeremiah had done wrong? Or was he just on the wrong side, but right about it all?

After Judah's defeat the finest young Jews were taken captive to Babylon. It wasn't long before they were commanded, along with the rest of the nation, to bow down before a huge image of Nebuchadnezzar. They refused and were thrown into a fiery furnace. (They could have rationalized, as some did in Japan during the war, "We were not worshipping in our hearts, we were only bending our bodies." Of course, the second commandment doesn't say anything about worshipping man-made images. It forbids bowing. "Thou shalt not bow down.")

A few years later Daniel, who rose to high positions of trust and authority, both in Babylon and Persia, disobeyed King Darius' order to pray only to him for thirty days." Daniel disobeyed the order, and was thrown in a den of lions.

In the New Testament John the Baptist meddled in the personal affairs of King Herod, and was beheaded. (Today's compromisers would rationalize, "If he had minded his own business, he could have had many more years to serve the Lord.")

The apostles defied the orders of the Sanhedrin, who had both religious and temporal authority, not to preach any more in the name of Jesus.

The Apostle John was exiled to Patmos for not giving full and proper obeisance to Roman authority.

The early church was often faced with the choice of being subservient to Roman authority, or obeying the Head of the Church, Jesus Christ, when the two were in conflict.

Where did that early twentieth century heresy come from that said God's people must always be compliant with man's government? Well, I guess the answer to that question is easy. From Satan himself. It is similar to what someone has said, "Satan is no happier than when people believe he does not exist."

With these questions with respect to the relationship that should exist between Christians and government, I go now to my message in opposition to the invasion and occupation of Iraq, broadcast on radio station WFAX, and printed in my periodical, Capitol Hill Voice.

STRAIGHT THINKING, PLAIN TALK, AND BOLD ACTION ON THE WAR AGAINST IRAQ

I'm not a Democrat or Republican, or a member of any political party. There's not a dime's worth of difference between the

Roosevelt socialist Democrats and the Rockefeller socialist Republicans.

I am an old fashioned George Mason-John Jay-Patrick Henry-Washington-J. Adams-Jefferson-Madison-Monroe-J.Q. Adams-Jackson conservative American patriot. I believe in revolution when it is necessary (that's how the U.S. got started), minding our own business among the nations of the world (America first isolationism), waging war against those who attack us, limited government, and Bill of Rights liberties for citizens.

The war against Iraq was contrary to all of the above. It was unnecessary, misguided, unwise, un-American, and unbiblical. Unbiblical? Yes! Remember the godly patriot Jeremiah? He warned Jehoiakim Bush not to go to war against Nebuchadnezzar Hussein, King of Babylon Iraq. (The parallelisms are astonishing.)

Iraq had nothing to do with the 9/11 terrorist attacks. It was right for us to go after Osama bin Laden in Afghanistan, but wrong to leave off chasing him down in order to chase Saddam Hussein.

Saddam Hussein had no weapons of mass destruction, much less plans to use them on us/US. It is simply wrong to go to war against an enemy who had not or could not threaten us in any way.

Prediction (in early 2003): This unnecessary war will turn in to an expensive, unmanageable, chaotic quagmire, and will prove to be one of the worst blunders ever made by a President in the history of the U.S.A. NOTE: I HAVE NOT HAD TO CHANGE MY MIND OR APOLOGIZE FOR ANY OF THESE PREDICTIONS AND ASSERTIONS MADE IN 2003 AND 2004. I WAS RIGHT ABOUT IT ALL FROM THE BEGINNING.

President Bush simply does not understand the Arab people of the world, especially Moslem Arabs. They are proud, accomplished people who do not want white men from the West invading, occupying and overrunning their countries telling them what to do, how to behave, what kind of government they should have, and who their leaders will be. They are offended, and they resent such condescending arrogance.

(Those who settled and built this country fought for liberty on the foundation of biblical truth. What monumental ignorance and presumption for anyone to think that our form of government can be given or imposed on people who possess a far different history and religion!)

Every know-it-all action by Westerners will generate ten retaliations by Iraqi Arabs and their friends in the Middle East, especially the Moslems.

Saddam Hussein, with all his faults and evils, knew how to manage his fractured society. He protected Christians and churches from Moslem crazies. He protected the Sunnis and Shias from each other. He meted out swift punishment to murderers, rapists, sodomites, burglars, robbers, muggers, looters, and thieves. I would much rather walk the streets of Baghdad at midnight under Saddam Hussein than the streets of Washington under Mayor Williams.

Now all of that totalitarian control is gone and the lawless are running the streets, towns, villages, and cities of Iraq.

Why didn't President Bush listen to the warnings of those who know that part of the world better than he does?

Yes, of course. Bush 43's fantasy that democracy will spread to Iraq, the entire Middle East and then to the world, is identical to his father 41's vision of a New World Order (a Skull and Bones doctrine).

The Bible does indeed predict a one world government in the last days before our Lord returns. It will be a world of satanically inspired "peace and safety." There is an irony here: Those nations of the world that at the present time maintain a semblance of law and order, such as Saudi Arabia—do not want our democracy with its divorce, dysfunctional families, out-of-control children, failed schools, fornication, pornography, unwed motherhood, abortion, and Hollywood style immorality, drunkenness, and crime.

America, repent before things get worse. Back to the Bible before it is too late. Return to constitutional representative government (not democracy.)

(Someone suggested recently that we take our Constitution to Iraq, and present it to the Iraqis as a gift, explaining, "Here is our Constitution. It served us well for about 200 years. But we don't use it or need it anymore. Here give it a try.")

* * * * *

President Bush has had much to say about an "axis of evil," made up of Iraq, Iran, and North Korea. Well, now that the war against Iraq has begun, I think it is clear that the most dangerous "axis of evil" in the world today consists of the United States of America, Israel, and the United Nations…capable together of perpetrating far more death, destruction, and misery upon the people of the world than President Bush's "axis of evil" ever dreamed of.

* * * * *

Now President Bush has come up with a "Road Map to Peace in the Middle East." But he forgot the first stop on his map. The first stop to any "road map to peace in the Middle East" must be Capitol Hill, where Congress must be told to terminate all U.S. giveaways and no-interest loans to Israel immediately. Support for Israel is the root cause of the 9/11 Twin Towers terrorist disaster, the war in Iraq, and continuing terrorism against the West worldwide. We have paid a high and terrible price for our stubborn, insane support for the anti-Christian, apartheid, immoral, terrorist nation of Israel.

* * * * *

Why yes! Of course! How were our elite rulers sure that Iraq had weapons of mass destruction? Easy! We supplied Saddam Hussein those weapons during the 1980s, when we were in love with him, and encouraging him in a bloody, brutal war against our former friends, Iran. We are a country gone crazy without God.

* * * * *

What right does any nation have to tell another sovereign nation what kind of and how many weapons it can have? How is it that Iraq is not permitted to have nuclear weapons, while Israel can keep several hundred nuclear weapons, without so much as a peep from the U.S. or U.N.?

* * * * *

Part of the high price that we are paying for our going to war against Iraq on behalf of Israel is that the lives of Americans around the world—tourists, businessmen, missionaries, all—are in constant jeopardy. And I resent it.

* * * * *

We are now the most proficient nation in the world in the business of destroying cities and nations, and then rebuilding them. There was a time when we were famous for building schools and hospitals and churches, and sending Bibles and books, teachers and missionaries, and good will to the people of the world. Now those activities are at an all-time low, while our elite rulers think it is God's will and their business to spend our finest and most expensive resources—especially lives—on destruction. God will judge us/US for our changing and misplaced priorities.

* * * * *

I said several times during the 2000 nominating process that one Bush in the White House was enough. And in 2003 I have not changed my mind.

* * * * *

George W. Bush has got to be thanking God every day...yes, maybe several times a day...that John F. Kerry is running against him for president. If the Democrats had put forth a halfway good candidate instead of this strange character, John F. Kerry, George W. Bush wouldn't have a chance. God have mercy on us! What have we come to in America when our choices are Bush, Kerry, and Nader? (There are others, of course. I think I will be writing in "Dale Crowley Jr.")

* * * * *

How can I as a Christian citizen who loves his country, and prays, and works hard for God's blessings upon it, vote for a man who is a member of a secret, occult, Satanic, society (Skull and Bones), who took our country into a costly war—not because he had to, but because he wanted to—and who is said to be the best friend anti-Christian Israel ever had in the White House?

* * * * *

If John Kerry wins this election, it will tell us more about America and Americans than about John Kerry...just as Bill Clinton's reelection victory in 1996 told us more about America and Americans than about Bill Clinton. We blame the elected politicians too much. We the voters and electors are the problem.

* * * * *

This is the Gospel radio ministry that is characterized by straight thinking, plain talk, and bold action. Just coming to the studios of radio station WFAX and sending out this kind of straight thinking and plain talk is—in and of itself—bold action.

* * * * *

You'll hear it first and perhaps only on THE KINGS BUSINESS radio program, and sometimes you'll hear it before it happens.

* * * * *

Your speaker is Dale Crowley Jr....on the wrong side of just about everything, but right about it all.

* * * * *

I'm Dale Crowley Jr.—out of step, out of harmony, out of tune, out of sync with just about everything new going on in Christianity and in American government and politics today.

CHAPTER 13

The Wisdom and Courage of Haviv Schieber—
"I Never Lost a Battle with My Jewish Brethren"

A *book could, and should be written about Haviv Schieber,*
one of the most unusual characters I ever knew.

I have noticed through the years that I am attracted to
"different" people, and that they are attracted to me. (No
offense meant, please, to my multitude of friends who are not
"different.") I think of Paul Fleming, founder of New Tribes
Mission, back in the days when he was persona non grata on
the campus of a large Christian college. I think of James
Graham, who was a pariah among Scofield dispensationalist
evangelical Christians.

And then there was Haviv Schieber, who did more for the
America he loved during 28 years of illegal alien status than
most of us natural born citizens do in a lifetime.

I met Haviv Schieber over coffee at the S&W cafeteria on
the WFAX radio station property in Falls Church Virginia—
"Tower Square"—in the summer of 1982, and buried him on
January 14, 1988—five and one-half years of pure exciting
adventure.

Haviv was born in Poland in 1913 into a rare anti-
Communist Jewish family about the same time and place as
Menachem Begin and Yitzhak Shamir. They were partners
in Zionism and terrorism, succeeding in driving the British
out of Palestine.

He was the first mayor of Beersheba, and was headed for
the top when he realized the evil of what his fellow East
European Marxist Jews were doing to the Palestinian people.

One day in 1956 when he arrived at the site of some
construction he was doing for the Tel Aviv Baptist Church,
he discovered a group of rabbis just completing their job of
destroying what he had built. He picked up a brick to hurl at

the rabbis when, he relates with confidence and emotion, he heard a voice from heaven, "This is not my way." Haviv dropped the brick, and right then and there believed Jesus Christ as his Lord and Saviour.

That was the beginning of 30 years of a lonely but successful struggle for truth and justice, righteousness and biblical principles of government, in Palestine, in Israel, and in the United States of America.

After arriving in this country on a speaking engagement, he fell in love with it, and stayed. For twenty-eight years he never had a green card; much less citizenship. Renouncing his Israeli citizenship, he became a man without a country.

Representative Jesse Helms of North Carolina introduced a bill to grant him citizenship, but Representative Elizabeth Holtzman of New York sabotaged it. Haviv then thwarted efforts to send him back to Israel and certain death many times.

It was Haviv Schieber, as an Israeli Jewish insider, so to speak, who assured me that Israel's attack on our ship sailing in the Mediterranean on June 8, 1967, the USS LIBERTY, was deliberate, and that it was the intent of Israel to sink the ship and kill every man on board. Why? Haviv explained that the Israeli generals were angry that the U.S. was gathering information on their conduct of the Six Day War...a war provoked by Israel's destroying a Palestinian source of water...because they were violating their agreement with the Pentagon about what they would not do in that war.

Haviv explained to me further that the fact that there never had been a Congressional investigation of the atrocity proved Israel's guilt. That is, if it had been an accident, or if it had been done by some other nation, it most certainly would have been investigated by Congress.

After nearly dying during surgery for colon and intestinal cancer in the summer of 1985, he informed his friends that he would be going to live with the Crowleys. We hadn't yet heard about it, but we remembered that Haviv Schieber was never wrong, and gave him the best places in our missionary hospitality home in Arlington, Virginia, to live the rest of his life. (Not one of his Jewish friends in the Washington area offered to help him in his need, yet I am the one who is accused of being an anti-Semite!) Haviv survived another two and one-half years until his death on New Year's Eve, December 31, 1987. He died penniless.

It was during those two and one-half years that Haviv encouraged me to begin the Focus on Israel radio program. He was a frequent guest speaker, often reading one of his favorite scriptures, the first chapter of Isaiah.

Several times before his death Haviv made me promise to conduct a Christian funeral for him. The Cherrydale Baptist Church, where he often attended with his friend and "angel," Daniel Hughes, set aside a grave site for him at the National Memorial Park cemetery. In accordance with his wishes we picked out a plain pine box casket at Murphy Funeral Home. Because he died on a holiday weekend, his remains were sent to the Arlington Hospital morgue to await burial on Monday, January 4th.

Incredibly, the day after his death, a rabbi from Rockville, Maryland—Schmuel Kaplan—threatened the Murphy Funeral Home and the Arlington Hospital with a lawsuit if they released Haviv's remains to me for the Christian funeral that I had promised him. The rabbi didn't know Haviv Schieber, had never met him, and Haviv had never had anything whatsoever to do with Rabbi Kaplan.

The rabbi's argument was that since Haviv Schieber was born of a Jewish mother he had to be buried in a Jewish cemetery with a Jewish service, or he would suffer in hell forever.

With the skillful and courageous work of an old friend of Haviv, attorney John Hemenway, we got the case on an Arlington County court docket. Judge Benjamin Kendrick ruled in our favor, against Rabbi Kaplan, on Wednesday, January 13, but the rabbi wouldn't sign the court order.

So we had to go back to court on Thursday the 14th where Judge Kendrick demanded the release of Haviv's remains for burial.

In the midst of my distress and grief the Arlington Hospital cajoled me in to signing an agreement that I would never mention the Arlington Hospital in connection with this matter.

I saw Haviv for the last time in the morgue. His remains were placed in the plain pine box, a funeral service was conducted at Murphy Funeral Home, and he was buried in the midst of a blizzard with many close friends gathered together around the grave site, around noon.

Friends, I have said all this as an introduction to the genius, the insight, the wisdom, and the courage of Haviv Schieber, as embodied in some of his most famous, or infamous sayings. These utterances of his were most often spoken in speeches that he would give, or even in conversation with old friends and new friends alike. They would show up in his writings—letters and articles—and, of course, on placards that he was fond of carrying wherever there might be a crowd.

As part fulfillment of my pledge never to let the world forget Haviv Schieber, I send out these most profound of his efforts to get people's attention, and to get out the truth. There is no better way to honor and to remember Haviv Schieber, or to get acquainted with him for the first time, than with the following.

The Wisdom and Courage of Haviv Schieber

"I have never lost a battle with my Jewish brethren...not in Poland, not in Germany, not in Israel, and not in her colony, the United States of America."

"My Jewish brethren love to hate. They cannot forgive. They are sick and need the doctor, Jesus, and the medicine, the Bible." (Note: Whenever Haviv Schieber made reference to being a Jew, or Jewish, he meant *ethnically* a Jew, Jewish. He was not a Jew religiously. He was a Christian.)

"If there was no such thing as anti-Semitism in the world, my

Jewish brethren would invent it. They have to have it to survive." (Note: It took me a while to figure this one out.)

"My Jewish brethren always go too far. Then comes the backlash."

"Zionism is Jewish Naziism."

"All what my Jewish brethren learned about oppressing the Palestinians, they learned from Hitler when they were in Germany."

"Naziism made me afraid to be a Jew. Zionism makes me ashamed to be a Jew."

Haviv Schieber's definition of Zionism: Rich U. S. Jews paying the way for the poor Jews of the world to go to Israel.

"The one thing that Israel hopes for more than anything else is that the blood of American soldiers will be spilled in the Middle East for her."

"There's no business like shoah business." ("Shoah" = "Holocaust")

"All the people of the world build monuments to their successes, their glories, and their heroes. Only my Jewish brethren build monuments to their defeats and shame."

Invariably, when people would meet Haviv for the first time, or following a speech, he would be asked about the authenticity of the "Protocols of the Elders of Zion." He always responded by putting his hands upward, palms up in a typical Jewish gesture, accompanied by his conclusion to the question, "Makes no difference. All has come true."

CHAPTER 14

In a Plain Pine Box,
Not a Shiny Aluminum Casket

⊷⇌◯⇋⊶

A best seller a few years back was *The High Cost of Dying.*
(*A takeoff on the expression, "The high cost of living."*)

It was nervy to write and publish such a book, since nothing will elicit more hard feelings, more vitriol, as far back as I can remember, than to question, much less cast the slightest aspersion on the modern "Christian civilization" ritual of $10,000, $20,000, even $50,000-$100,000 funerals.

Surely it is important in times of the greatest of all losses and griefs, not only to show respect for the departed, but in some great way to express our gratitude and love.

Still, I just can't understand it fully. We Christians like to go to the Bible for everything. Well, the closest thing in Bible times comparable to the time and money spent on burying the dead today were the multi-million dollar extravaganzas for dead pharaohs—building the pyramids, mummifying the bodies, and hiding the deceased away deep inside the pyramids through elaborate passageways, with all manner of precious metals and other expensive objects.

But God's specific instructions for His people in the matter of burying the dead cannot be found in the Bible. What we do see is a long history of respect for the deceased's remains, the chiseling of a sepulcher in a hillside, expensive cloth in which the remains were wrapped, and all kinds of oils, perfumes, and preservatives applied to both the remains and the cloth. There are indications that burial was to be as soon as possible, on the same day as death if possible.

I would like to cite just one ideal, most proper biblical burial. God buried Moses, I'm sure in a most respectful, efficient, and simple manner. I can't imagine God embalm-

ing Moses. If anyone deserved the best, it was Moses. And he got it.

But woe to the preacher who dares to make even the slightest mention of the lack of biblical instruction and example, or the need for simplicity—reverent simplicity—in the matter of the burial of the dead.

So where do we go from here?

I go back to the man whom God sent in to my life who was always so simple, so sincere, so profound, and always so right about everything—Haviv Schieber.

I was deeply moved and admonished when my Christian friend, who was a Jew, told me plainly and clearly one day that when he died he wanted me to bury him with a Christian service, on the same day of his death, in a pine box.

My immediate response was one of disbelief, "Is that possible, Haviv?" I only showed my ignorance about such important things. (But I learned that plain pine boxes are on display and sold by funeral homes, and that cemeteries do accommodate such requests with "same day service." I also discovered that pine boxes must be placed in a concrete liner, just as shiny aluminum caskets must.)

I said, "Sure, Haviv, I promise."

I didn't ask any questions then, but I did do some thinking about death, funerals, and burial.

First, Haviv knew that he would die penniless. And he knew that none of his friends had much money either. He was being thoughtful.

Second, Haviv knew well the biblical truth that our physical remains, worth nothing after death, must remain behind while our eternal spirit is received by our God and Saviour. (On the evening of his death, I witnessed Haviv, after he had lain motionless for a few seconds, suddenly open his eyes wide, look upward with a glorious smile on his face. I thought he was coming back to life, but now I know that he was getting his reception into the presence of his Lord and Saviour Jesus Christ. I have no idea exactly what he was seeing, but I know it was wonderful.)

And lastly, I sincerely believe that what Haviv had requested of me was right, and biblical, though contrary to the American way of death.

So I decided then and there that out of respect to my dear departed friend, and in keeping with what I know about the biblical pattern of death, funerals, and burials, that I will follow the example of Haviv Schieber.

I will be buried, without embalming, if possible on the same day that I die, in a plain pine box. The only service will be at grave side. It is in my will.

Now read a message that I dared to prepare for radio broadcast, and which was printed in The Capitol Hill Voice in 1996.

Readers of *Capitol Hill Voice* know by now to expect very unusual articles. The purpose of this unusual article is not to cause alarm or distress (though the pro-Israel cultists will be glad when I'm gone), but to give glory to God and to make preparation for events sure to take place.

I have been living for 6, 8, or 10 years (or longer) with a completely (100 percent) blocked right main heart artery, the one that supplies blood to one-third of heart muscles. If this blockage had developed over a short period of time it would have meant a heart attack, and possibly death.

But through the years God performed His own bypass operation by putting in place a countless number of tiny blood vessels that connect my blocked right artery with the right chamber of my heart.

God did not miraculously unblock the blocked right artery, but He did miraculously connect the blocked artery with the heart.

So I praise the Lord that I am less in need of bypass surgery in 1996 than in 1990 when this condition was discovered.

Now I have no way of knowing whether my heart condition will cause my death, but I can be certain that if I am not caught up in the rapture of the church (still a few years in the future, after the Great Tribulation), God will allow something to transfer me from this earthly sphere to His presence.

That means that a dead body will be left behind for my family and friends to take care of, and I want *Capitol Hill Voice* readers to know that I have done my best to express my will on this important matter sensibly and clearly.

I have studied my Bible on the subject of burial enough to know that the custom in Bible times was to bury a person's remains as soon as possible after death, usually the same day or the next day. It is pretty much a matter of custom and/or our personal wishes.

My personal will is that I be buried as Israelites were buried in Bible times, and as my dear Christian friend Haviv Schieber (who was an Ashkenazi Jew) was buried—within 24 hours after death, in a plain pine box casket. (His burial was delayed.)

State laws and cemeteries provide for such burial. There will be no embalming, no cremation, no long wait for a funeral service, no expensive casket. The only service will be at graveside. (If I die during a holiday season, my remains will have to be kept in a morgue until the cemetery gets back to work…a little adjustment made necessary and possible only in these modern times!) Funeral homes always keep a supply of pine box caskets for these kinds of burials.

Finally I can only beg that my family and friends will honor my will in the matter of my burial. It is written in my will.

If you attend a funeral in which these conditions do not obtain, it could be that you have attended the funeral of someone other than Dale Crowley Jr.

"So also is the resurrection of the dead. It is sown in corruption; it is raised in incorruption. It is sown in dishonor; it is raised in glory. It is sown in weakness; it is raised in power. It is sown a natural body; it is raised a spiritual body. There is a natural body, and there is a spiritual body." I Corinthians 15:42-44.

CHAPTER 15

The Apostle Paul Not Qualified in Christianity Today

Dear friends, as a believer in the divine inspiration and inerrancy of the Bible, I have always been skeptical of all the rules and regulations, policies and polities, and doctrines and traditions characteristic of churches and denominations, and other religious (often Christian) organizations that cannot be found in the Bible. Such organizations include even mission boards, the name given to those organizations that are devoted to the specialized tasks of recruiting, training, approving, and sending missionaries to foreign countries.

A good example of such unbiblical, extra-biblical systems is the new sacrosanct system of decision making known as democracy. Many politicians are eager to spread democracy to the nations of the world, and many Christians boast that their church's government is democratic. But democratic government, either for nations or for churches, cannot be found the word of God.

I had two major scrapes with this kind of error when I was a young man called of God to the mission field of Japan. First, the church where I grew up on Capitol Hill in Washington, D.C., and which assured me and my wife that they would be one of our foreign missionary supporters, voted democratically one Wednesday night in 1952, "No." Following that, two mission boards decided that they, for various reasons could not sponsor us for missionary service in Japan at that time. (We were too young and didn't have sufficient college and seminary education. But we went on to Japan in 1952, and witnessed one of the greatest works of God and outpourings of His Spirit in postwar Japan—growing, prospering and multiplying even to this day.)

With that background, you can understand why I glee-fully responded to an imaginary letter to Missionary Saul Paul, who already was the greatest missionary in the history of the church, explaining why he could not be approved by their board for missionary service. I was inspired to improve on the "first draft" of this letter, which I first read in the 1950s, and which I send out in this message. I never knew who the author of the "first draft" was. If anyone of my listeners or readers knows, I will be much indebted to know better who shares the title with me, "On the wrong side of just about everything, but right about it all."

The imaginary letter of rejection from a first century mission board to Missionary Saul Paul has always given me pleasure. I read a shorter version of the letter many years ago, and then embellished it with a few more incidents from Paul's "unorthodox" ministerial and missionary career.

It is not my intention to cast unwarranted reflection upon those sincere Christian organizations that are trying to do their best for the Kingdom of God. But the fact remains that a lot of high powered organizational structure, high tech procedures, Madison Avenue style promotion, and man-made requirements have all but ruled out the Holy Spirit of God from any role in the accomplishment of spiritual goals and evangelization.

The first chapter of one of Paul's letters—First Corinthians—makes it clear that God will bless and use anyone, in or out of organized religion, if that person will simply yield himself to Him.

The setting for this imaginary letter is this: Paul has just completed some twenty years of successful missionary work. He is now contemplating continuing his ministry to the nations of the world with a measure of prestige and security by gaining the approval and sponsorship of a mission board.

What follows is the reply of the mission board to the application of Missionary Saul Paul.

Dear Rev. Paul:

We recently received an application from you for service under our board. It is our policy to be as frank and open-minded as possible with all our applicants. We have made an exhaustive survey in your case, and to be plain, we are surprised that you have been able to pass as a *bonafide* missionary.

We are told that you are afflicted with a severe eye difficulty. This is certain to be an insuperable handicap to an effective ministry. Our board requires 20-20 vision.

At Antioch, we learn, you opposed Dr. Simon Peter, an esteemed denominational worker, and actually rebuked him publicly. You stirred up so much trouble at Antioch that a special board meeting had to be convened in Jerusalem. We cannot condone such behavior.

Do you think it appropriate for a missionary to do part-time work? We hear that you are making tents on the side. In a letter to the church at Phillipi you admitted that they were the only church supporting you. We wonder, "Why?"

Is it true that you have a jail record? Certain brethren report that you did two years time at Caesarea and were imprisoned in Rome. Our board cannot risk such incidents.

You made so much trouble for the businessmen at Ephesus that they refer to you as "the man who turned the world upside down." Sensationalism has no place in missions. We also deplore the lurid "over-the-wall-in-a-basket" episode at Damascus.

We are appalled at your obvious lack of conciliatory behavior. Diplomatic men are not stoned and dragged out of the city gate, or assaulted by mobs. Have you ever suspected that gentler words might gain you more friends? I enclose a copy of Dalius Carnegus' book, *How to Win Jews and Influence Greeks*.

In one of your letters you refer to yourself as "Paul the aged." Our new mission policies do not envisage a surplus of superannuated applicants.

We understand that you are given to fantasies and dreams. At Troas you saw "a man of Macedonia," and at another time you "were caught up into the third heaven," and even claimed "the Lord stood by" you. We reckon that more realistic and practical minds are needed in the task of world evangelization.

You have caused much trouble everywhere you have gone. You opposed the honorable women at Berea, and the leaders of your own nationality at Jerusalem. If a man cannot get along with his own people, how can he serve foreigners? You admit that while you were serving time at Rome, "all forsook you." Good men are not left friendless. Three fine brothers by the names of Diotrophes, Demas, and Alexander the coppersmith, have written us to the effect that it is impossible for them to cooperate with either you or your program. We also know that you had a bitter quarrel with a fellow missionary named Barnabas. Harsh words do not further God's work.

You have written many letters to churches where you formerly have been pastor. In one of these letters you accused a church member of living with his father's wife, and you caused the whole church to feel bad, and the poor fellow was expelled. You spend too much time talking about "the second coming of Christ." Your letters to the people of Thessalonica were almost entirely devoted to this theme. Put first things first from now on.

Your ministry has been far too flighty be successful. First Asia Minor, then Macedonia, then Greece, then Italy, and now you are talking about a wild goose chase into Spain. Concentration is more important than dissipation of one's powers. You cannot win the whole world by yourself. You are just one little Paul.

In a recent sermon you said, "God forbid that I should glory in anything save the cross of Christ." It appears to us that you are not an organizational man. You could very well be proud of some religious organization, its heritage, its program, its budget, and, of course, the World Council of Churches.

Your sermons are much too long for the time. Once you talked until after midnight, and a young man was so sleepy that he fell out of a window and broke his neck. "Stand up, speak up, then shut up" is our advice.

Dr. Luke reports that you are a thin little bald man, frequently sick, and ways so agitated over your churches that you sleep poorly. He reports that you pad around the house, praying half the night. A healthy mind in a robust body is our ideal for all applicants.

You wrote recently to Timothy that you had "fought a good fight." Fighting is hardly a recommendation for a missionary. "No fight is a good fight" is our motto.

No, Rev. Paul, if we considered your application we would be breaking every precedent and established policy of our Board. But rather than simply refuse you we thought we would write this more detailed, helpful letter.

Sincerely yours, The Board.

CHAPTER 16

It Doesn't Pay to be Right in Christianity Today

It's time now to look at what happens financially to the preacher and teacher who dares to be "on the wrong side of just about everything, but right about it all."

As well as having monetary and financial connotations, "pay" also has abstract meanings, such as "to be advantageous," "to be worthwhile," "to be beneficial," and "to stand one in good stead." A third meaning is most certainly spiritual; that is, "to be rewarded and blessed of God," and "to lay up treasures in heaven."

In this chapter I intend to convey all three meanings. Some will judge "It Doesn't Pay" to be cynical, even sarcastic and unkind. Well, it needs to be said, and here is a good place to say it: In Christianity today we are afraid and unwilling to be cynical, sarcastic, and judgmental, when those kinds of expressions are called for.

Noah built a ship—not fame and fortune—telling an ungodly world what they didn't want to hear, and building a ship. And a year on board in the midst of rain, flood, and smelly animals wasn't pleasant for him, his wife and family. All eight of them no doubt had feelings and voiced expressions that were 100 percent human.

Elijah suffered much inconvenience, deprivation, and affliction because of a wicked king and queen, and eventually spoke unkind words to the king, and sarcastic words to his false prophets.

Jeremiah paid a terrible price for his cynicism, sarcasm, and for being on the wrong side of political correctness in Judah.

In the New Testament the Apostle Paul's inspired writings contain instances of cynicism, sarcasm, and criticism.

There is always a measure of truth and propriety in irony, cynicism, and in being judgmental.

Now read what happens to the preacher who has dared to teach and broadcast the truth on various topics for over 50 years.

**IN CHRISTIANITY TODAY IT DOES NOT PAY
TO BE RIGHT
IN CHRISTANIITY TODAY IT DOES NOT PAY
TO BE SELF-CONFIDENT
IN CHRISTIANITY TODAY IT DOES NOT
PAY TO EXPOSE ERROR**

Fifty years ago a famous evangelist began announcing, before every city wide crusade, "This crusade will be the beginning of a nationwide revival." I said, "Not so. America will continue its downward plunge into sin, lawlessness, and rebellion against God, leading to divine judgment." The false prophet raked in millions, while I remained a poor preacher and missionary. In Christianity in America today it doesn't pay to be right.

Over forty years ago I began exposing the errors and heresies of Darby/Scofield/Lindsey dispensationalism. The dispensational teachers continue to this day to prosper with the support of their "itching ears" followers. I remain the poor preacher and teacher of historical biblical sound doctrine. In Christianity in America today it doesn't pay to be right.

Following the Supreme Court's infamous decision in 1963, preachers and politicians began promising, "Give me your money and your votes and I'll restore voluntary prayer and Bible reading to our schools." I declared boldly, "The Supreme Court has not banned voluntary prayer and Bible reading on school grounds." The deceivers got their money and their votes by the millions. The preacher who told the truth remains poor. In Christianity in America today it doesn't pay to be right.

Throughout the latter half of this century I have denounced the popular "easy believism" and "health and wealth" gospels preached by many of America's most famous purveyors of sweet medicine.

These con artists have profited hugely, while the preacher of the Gospel as Jesus preached it remains poor. In Christianity in America today it doesn't pay to be right.

As you have read in a preceding chapter, I began exposing the fallacies of "creation science" and the "two-model approach" 25 years ago. But while the promoters of these flawed concepts received contributions from Christians by the millions, this straight-thinking, truth-telling preacher remains poor. In Christianity in America today it doesn't pay to be right.

In the early 1980s a group of sensationalist charlatans in Oklahoma began a nationwide money making scheme based on a deception they named, "The Jupiter Effect." They published a leaflet showing the planets lined up in a straight line, which would cause catastrophes on earth on March 10, 1982. With the help of the U.S. Naval Observatory I exposed this hoax. But while the charlatans made millions on their sideshow hoax, the preacher who exposed it remained poor. In Christianity in America today it doesn't pay to be right.

In the mid-1980s another dispensationalist pre-tribulation rapture "Christian" quack published a booklet listing 88 reasons why Jesus would rapture the church in 1988. He sold several million copies of his fraudulent unsound doctrine to American Christians. I denounced his error publicly and boldly, but while he raked in greenbacks by the thousands, this poor preacher got nothing. In Christianity in America today it doesn't pay to be right.

Through the years I have given many biblical reasons why the modern nation of Israel is an "unfruitful work of darkness." (Ephesians 5:11) Year after year, month after month, week after week I am proved to be right. Yet preachers and teachers across the land who are devotees of the cult of Israel are assured of millions of dollars of regular support from gullible Christians who are in love with anti-Christ, anti-Christian Israel. And all the while this poor preacher who dares to tell the truth about Israel is despised and criticized. A Christian broadcast executive tried to persuade my radio station to throw me off the air because I was against Israel! In Christianity in America today it doesn't pay to be right.

In both 1990 and 2003 I denounced the Bushs' (41's and 43's) wars against Iraq as unnecessary, un-American, immoral, and unbiblical. I further proclaimed boldly that Bush 43's war would prove to be one of the greatest blunders ever committed by a President of the United States of America. From the beginning I predicted chaos, confusion, and great loss of life and money. I condemned the loathsome policy of passing the cost of such follies on to our children and grandchildren. I did not have to change my mind or apologize for being wrong. I was right from before the beginning of the war. What did l get for being right and preaching the truth in Washington with boldness and authority? Half of my contributors forsook me. What did the "war-mongering," Israel-first false prophets get? Their millions. (This war was fought at the behest of Israel...many of my fellow evangelicals are rejoicing that the U.S.A. can spend its lives and money on behalf of Israel.) In Christianity in America today it doesn't pay to be right. But it is far greater riches to be on the side of right and truth than to profit from error and deception.

"The time will come when they will not endure sound doctrine, but they, having itching ears, will heap to themselves teachers... who shall turn away their ears from the truth." (II Tim. 4:3-4) That time has come. I am thankful for you who love and support sound doctrine.

Please help me circulate this book far and wide.

ABOUT THE AUTHOR

⋆⇌⋆

Born the son of a militant fundamentalist Baptist pastor and evangelist in 1928, Dale Crowley Jr. was exposed to many twentieth century struggles between truth and error. Curiosity and skepticism were traits from childhood, with a deep respect for what is right, factual, and scientific.

His father's offensives against evolutionism at Baylor University in the 1920s, against doctrinal error in Jonesboro, Arkansas, with nearly the loss of his life in the 1930s, and against "wickedness in high places" in Washington, D.C. in the 1940s, all had a great impact on his ministry, which began in 1950 as pastor of the Berea Baptist Church of Elizabeth City, N. C.

Gospel radio broadcasting was a major daily activity in the Crowley family in Texas, Arkansas, Washington, Maryland, and Virginia, as his father was one of America's radio broadcasting pioneers. Thus immersed from childhood in this new way to send out the word of God, Dale Jr. was inspired to prepare and broadcast thousands of true-to-the-Bible messages on many, many topics, even while employed and engaged in various pursuits, including such things as linguistic research, Christian school administration, and teaching.

Mr. Crowley and his wife Mary served as missionaries in post-war Japan. In the 1960s he was employed by the University of Hawaii and Hawaii Department of Education as a language and linguistics researcher, and as a developer of teaching and learning materials for English, Japanese, and several Pacific and Asian languages. In the 1980s and 1990s he was president of National Heritage Foundation.

His preparation for this broad spectrum of tasks consisted of undergraduate work in Bible and Greek at Bob Jones University, and graduate work at three schools: The University of Oklahoma Graduate School (Wycliffe Bible Translators Summer Institute of Linguistics), Waseda University Graduate School in Tokyo, and the Georgetown University Graduate School in Washington. He holds a Master of Science degree in Applied Linguistics.

His radio broadcasting, which began in the late 1940s when he was guest speaker on his father's program, form the core of this publication. After returning to his hometown, Washington, D.C., in 1976, he concentrated on the radio broadcasting part of his busy life.

These messages...many embodied in sixteen chapters...often went through various stages—extemporaneous, comprehensive notes, and carefully written manuscripts for publication. Mr. Crowley figures that he has made around 7,000 trips to the studios of radio station WFAX to broadcast his always unusual messages.

The Crowleys, celebrating their fifty-fifth wedding anniversary in 2005, live in Virginia. They have five children, grandchildren and great-grandchildren, the number of whom changes from year to year. They are members of the Believers Baptist Church (independent) of Leesburg, Virginia, where their son-in-law Terry Overstreet is pastor.